Hidden PROFITS
In Your Back Yard

by
Hugh Carter

Exciting new strategies for creating
wealth in the 21st Century

© 2003 Carter Investment Group. All rights reserved.

No part of this material may be reproduced by any means, electronically or mechanically, without prior written permission of the author.

Cover design:
   William Bushell, Summer House Studio
   email: summerhouse@pacificcoast.net
   web site: www.pacificcoast.net/~summerhouse

Editors:
   Eileen Leddy
   email: eleddy@home.com
   Maurine Karagianis
   email: maurinekaragianis@shaw.ca

Manuscript assistance, transcription, desktop publisher and web master:
   Pat Dunget, Custom Office Services
   email: patd@shaw.ca

Carter, Hugh, 1953 -
Hidden Profits In Your Back Yard
ISBN 1-55212-575-0
1 Real Estate Investment   I.Title
HD1382.5 C37 2003 332.63'24 C2003-910705-6

Published by D.H. Carter
Website: www.dhcarter.com

To the Reader
...
"The New Millenium Entrepreneur"

Acknowledgements

I would like to thank the following people for their painstaking efforts in making this book possible:

Bill Barazzuol for his initial encouragement and editing of my early manuscripts.

Pat Dunget for many years of helping me write and rewrite my manuscripts.

Bill Bushell for his cover design and book formatting.

Eileen Leddy for the magic in her editing.

Table Of Contents

Acknowledgements ---------------------------------- **4**

Preface --- **10**

Chapter 1 - The Changing Real Estate Scene --- **14**
Who Is The New Millennium Real
    Estate Entrepreneur? ------------------------- 15

Chapter 2 - Urban Sprawl ------------------------- **18**
The Facts -- 18
Smart Growth ----------------------------------- 19
Myths About Infill Housing --------------------- 20
The Facts About Infill Housing ----------------- 22

Chapter 3 - Real Estate Overview --------------- **24**
Six Real Estate Categories --------------------- 24
What Makes Real Estate Values Rise? --------- 25
What Makes Real Estate Values Fall? ---------- 27
Traditional Types Of Residential
    Real Estate Investments --------------------- 29

Chapter 4 - Become An Expert ----------------- **32**
Acquire Knowledge ----------------------------- 34
Conquer Fear ------------------------------------ 35
Take Action -------------------------------------- 36
Maintain Discipline And Focus ----------------- 37

Chapter 5 - Getting Started --------------------- **40**
The Realtor -------------------------------------- 40
The Lawyer -------------------------------------- 41
The Home Designer ----------------------------- 42
The Home Inspector ----------------------------- 42
The Surveyor ------------------------------------ 43
Surveyor's Site Plan Before --------------------- 44

Surveyor's Site Plan After ------------------------ 45
The Contractor ---------------------------------- 46
The Municipal Planner --------------------------- 47
The Banker -------------------------------------- 47
The Accountant ---------------------------------- 48

Chapter 6 - Finding Diamonds In The Rough ------------------------------------- 50
Three Hypothetical Cases ------------------------ 50
Finding Diamonds In The Rough --------------- 52
  For Beginners ---------------------------------- 52
Watch Out For Sharks! -------------------------- 53
More About Tools -------------------------------- 53
Finding Diamonds In The Rough For Experts 55
The Feasibility Study ---------------------------- 57
Feasibility Study Worksheet - Example 1 ----- 58
Feasibility Study Worksheet - Example 2 ----- 60
Feasibility Study Worksheet - Example 3 ----- 62
Feasibility Study Worksheet - Example 4 ----- 64
Hidden Profits On Main Street Video ----------- 66

Chapter 7 - Types Of Infill Housing Lots ---- 68
A: The Dual Neighbour Corner Lot ------------- 69
B: The Dual Neighbour Split Lot ---------------- 70
C: The Side-By-Side Strata Duplex Lot -------- 71
D: The Front And Back Strata Duplex Lot ---- 72
E: The Up And Down Strata Duplex Lot ------- 73
F: The Panhandle Lot --------------------------- 74
G: Dual Neighbour Panhandle Lot, Type 1 ---- 75
H: Dual Neighbour Panhandle Lot, Type 2 ---- 76
I: Dual Neighbour Panhandle Lot, Type 3 ---- 77
J: The Side-By-Side Double Lot ---------------- 78
K: The Front And Back Double Lot ------------- 79
L: The Strata Lot -------------------------------- 80

Chapter 8 - Secondary Suites -------------------- 82
Opportunity Knocks ----------------------------- 82
The Fundamentals ------------------------------ 83

Table Of Contents

Great Way To Start ------------------------------ 84
ROI (Return On Investment) --------------------- 85
Types Of Secondary Units ----------------------- 86

Chapter 9 - The Opportunity --------------------- **88**
Demographics And Statistics -------------------- 88
The Crystal Ball -------------------------------- 89
The Sleeping Giant ------------------------------ 90
Where To Look ---------------------------------- 90
The Facts Of Life -------------------------------- 91
The Changing Household ----------------------- 92
Population Explosion Graph -------------------- 93
LOIs (Leading Opportunity Indicators) --------- 93
The Canadian National Population Table ----- 94
Southern Ontario ------------------------------- 95
Southwestern Alberta -------------------------- 95
Southwestern British Columbia --------------- 96
Provincial Statistics ---------------------------- 97
Sleepers --- 97
The Canadian Housing Statistics Table ------- 98

Chapter 10 - The Purchase -------------------- **100**
The Offer --------------------------------------- 100
The Title Search ------------------------------- 101
The Closing ------------------------------------ 102

Chapter 11 - The Neighbourhood ------------- **104**
Letter To Neighbours -------------------------- 105
Conducting A Neighbourhood Meeting -------- 106
Letters Of Support From Neighbours --------- 108
Disapproval Letter From A Neighbour -------- 109

Chapter 12 - The Development Process --- **112**
The Zoning ------------------------------------- 112
The Zoning Bylaw Regulation Handbook ----- 112
The Zoning Bylaw Regulation Chart ---------- 113
The Rezoning Process ------------------------- 114
The Subdivision Process ---------------------- 116

Development Costs ---------------------------- 117
The Building Permit --------------------------- 118
Canadian Home Builders' Association -------- 119
Strata Title --------------------------------- 119
The Variables -------------------------------- 121
The Product ---------------------------------- 122

Chapter 13 - The Residential Mortgage ---- 124
Mortgage Definition --------------------------- 124
Mortgage Clauses ----------------------------- 125
The Key Components Of
  A Residential Mortgage ---------------------- 126
Canadian Versus American Mortgages ------- 127
Interest Rate Comparisons -------------------- 127
The Interest Rate Comparison Table ---------- 129
The Investment Strategy ---------------------- 129
Mortgage Books ------------------------------- 130
Overview ------------------------------------- 130

Chapter 14 - The Financing ------------------- 132
Plan A: Residential Mortgage ----------------- 132
Plan B: Applying For A Mortgage -------------- 133
Plan C: Home Equity -------------------------- 136
Plan D: PLC (Personal Line Of Credit) -------- 137
Plan E: RRSP (Registered Retirement
  Savings Plan) ------------------------------- 137
Plan F: Don't Over Extend --------------------- 138
The Final Word ------------------------------- 138

Chapter 15 - The Sale ---------------------- 140
Turnover ------------------------------------- 140
The Target Market ---------------------------- 141
Selling Your Projects ------------------------ 144

Chapter 16 - The Real Estate Pension Plan 146
How To Get There From Here ------------------ 146
The Renter ----------------------------------- 146

Table Of Contents

The Owner -- 147
The Five Year Plan ------------------------------- 148
Option 1: Secondary Suite --------------------- 148
Option 2: Equity Access Investment ---------- 148
The Bottom Line --------------------------------- 149

The Conclusion ----------------------------------- **151**

Appendix A-Generic Zoning Bylaw
   Regulation Chart ------------------------------ 154
Appendix B-Generic Zoning Map -------------- 155
Appendix C-Generic Rezoning Flow Chart --- 156
Appendix D-Generic Subdivision Flow Chart 158
Appendix E-Feasibility Study Worksheet ----- 160
Appendix F-Preliminary Check-List ----------- 162
Appendix G-Canadian Housing Statistics
   Table -- 163
Appendix H - Home Buyers Plan Request
   To Withdraw Funds From An RRSP -------- 164

The Glossary -------------------------------------- **165**

Disclaimer -- **170**

**Praise for "Hidden Profits In Your
   Back Yard"** -------------------------------------- **171**

Order Form -- **172**

PREFACE

In 1986, my career as a real estate entrepreneur began with the purchase of a revenue-producing duplex. I had often wondered if dealing with tenants, property management, leaky faucets and late night calls would be worthwhile. Then, two things started to work in my favour: inflation began to drive the value of my properties up well beyond my expectations and Revenue Canada announced the cancellation of the $100,000 capital gains exemption. It was time to sell!

During that period of my life, I also bought and sold several distressed properties. By 1990, my real estate ventures had earned me a total of $150,000 in cash and equity. That amount was four times higher than my average yearly wage had ever been. What a wake-up call! I put up with the grind of being a landlord and paying taxes on my profits because I realized I could continue to make good money. I saw my future in real estate—life was good.

Then something happened that changed my view forever. My marriage failed and I needed to find a new place to live—but didn't want an apartment. Instead, I decided to purchase another house.

My search led to a small house on a corner lot. The realtor told me the house and lot had duplex potential. We struck a deal quickly. I went down to the municipal hall immediately to make inquiries about duplexing. Once the information

Preface

gathering stage was complete, I began the rezoning and subdividing process. It took some time and effort but in the end the project received the municipal stamp of approval.

I lived in the existing home while I built the new unit. Upon completion, the duplex was strata titled. I sold the units separately, structuring each sale as my principle residence. In just seven months, I had made $80,000, tax free.

It requires fortitude to make this kind of commitment, to leave your comfort zone and take control of your own destiny. It's not for everyone. But, if you possess the right information, the kind of information that gives you the confidence and courage to take action, anything is possible. We all have the ability to be creative, use our imaginations, develop decision-making skills and learn. Ask yourself this question, "How long do I want to continue working hard every day, taking direction from a supervisor and then turning all that hard-earned money over to the bank or CCRA (Canadian Customs and Revenue Agency)?"

This book offers an alternative to that way of life and a realistic approach to wealth-building for the average Canadian. It provides all the information you need to be a successful real estate entrepreneur. Sixteen easy-to-follow chapters demonstrate the straight-forward steps you can take to buy and sell residential real estate for profit. You will learn proven ways to build cash and equity through infill housing development. Applying the techniques from this book, tried and tested by myself and others, can help you accomplish five important things:

Hidden Profits In Your Back Yard

- Independence for you and your family
- Employment for others
- A new tax base for your community
- More affordable housing
- A stimulated economy
- Protecting the environment from urban sprawl

I wrote this book to enable you to uncover opportunities to create wealth through a very basic, traditional commodity—residential real estate. Tailor the information to suit your needs. As you read this book, make notes and start a journal. Have your own team of experts answer your questions, and visit my web site at www.dhcarter.com.

I dedicate this book to YOU—my peers—the New Millennium Real Estate Entrepreneurs. May you grow financially secure by following the suggestions offered in this book.

Chapter 1

The Changing Real Estate Scene

Chapter 1
The Changing Real Estate Scene

The days of buying a home or revenue property and watching as inflation drove the value of that property up, up, up are gone, gone, gone. Yet, it is still possible to make a profit in the real estate market. In fact, we're heading into what may be some of the most profitable years real estate entrepreneurs will ever see. The time is right to seize the opportunities for profit that exist today, in residential land subdivided during the last century.

After 1945, renewed prosperity fueled massive new housing starts. Veterans returning home from overseas, and a steady influx of new immigrants, marked a new beginning. Young families abounded and jobs were plentiful. Development was steady and there seemed to be no end in sight: cities, suburbs, and small towns prospered. Not only did this period of growth mark the onset of the "Baby Boom" but it also spawned a new phenomenon: the beginning of urban sprawl. In the 21st century real estate market, opportunities for average Canadians exist in revisiting the urban neighbourhoods that mushroomed after WWII.

Unlike the cost of developing raw land, the cost of re-developing those older lots is minimal because all of the infrastructure such as roads, power, gas, sewers, water, cablevision and telephone services are already in place. In addition, many municipalities are relaxing rigid bylaws and making it easier to develop smaller, non-traditional infill building lots.

The Changing Real Estate Scene

Residential infill housing development creates more useable living space in populated areas. It also provides a solution to the housing crisis that currently exists in our country. The New Millennium Real Estate Entrepreneur (the infill housing developer) can seize the opportunities for wealth-building that lie in creating new infill housing on post-war properties. There is an added bonus of helping to protect forest, farm and wet lands from urban sprawl.

Who Is The New Millennium Real Estate Entrepreneur?

You are! No matter who you are or what you do, the information in this book will help you uncover opportunities to create the financial freedom you deserve. It will benefit:

- Average working Canadians who think they may never be able to afford to own a home
- Home-owners interested in the lucrative field of residential infill developing
- Real estate entrepreneurs looking for a blue chip real estate investment vehicle free of tenants, maintenance, management and long-term risk
- Realtors willing to focus on new opportunities for themselves and their clients
- Financial planners seeking sound opportunities to kick-start their clients' investment portfolios

Hidden Profits In Your Back Yard

Right now, millions of Canadians are trading their valuable time for money in the form of a full-time job, taxable by CCRA (Canada Customs and Revenue Agency) in a middle to high tax bracket. A small minority are trading time for part-time careers that are tax free or capital gains exempt, creating wealth equal to three or four full-time jobs. They are the infill housing developers.

Don't get me wrong. Jobs are important. They help define our purpose in life, build self-esteem and generate cash flow. More importantly, a job produces the taxable income necessary to qualify for a residential mortgage. The banks love hard-working, upstanding citizens who pay lots of taxes. The way they see it, if you're doing well enough to pay taxes then you're doing well enough to qualify for a mortgage. That is why banks love lending money, by the bucket loads, to buyers in the residential housing market.

The challenge is to capitalize on that banking feature, and on other related opportunities, to create a new and rewarding career and join the ranks of the New Millennium Real Estate Entrepreneurs.

Chapter 2

Urban Sprawl

Chapter 2
Urban Sprawl

In the coming years, urban sprawl will become the leading housing, social, and environmental challenge in Canada and the United States. The issue of urban sprawl has been threatening to explode for more than twenty years. Its time has finally arrived and it will continue to receive top media attention.

The by-products of sprawl are haphazard growth, traffic congestion, air pollution, overcrowded highways and lost forests, farm or wet lands. They are serious issues which are forcing us to reconsider where and how we build. But build we must, because population growth at the present time in North America, and indeed in the world, is well over 1% per year.

The Facts

The United States is losing over three million acres every year to urban sprawl. Metro Washington, D.C. is losing 28 acres a day to sprawl. In Phoenix AR., sprawl is creeping into the desert at the rate of one acre per hour.

Several recent studies in the United States have concluded that the land mass consumed by new development is outstripping population growth by 300%. For instance, the Puget Sound area of Washington State had a 36% increase in population between 1970 and 1990, while the land consumption for development increased by

Urban Sprawl

87%. Kansas City's population grew 30% between 1960 and 1990, but developed land increased by 110%. Between 2000 and 2005 the population of Las Vegas will double. What will happen to the desert as the city limits sprawl into it?

Any city in Canada that is now experiencing a 1% population growth per annum will see its population double this century. British Columbia's Fraser Valley and Ontario's Golden Horseshoe are Canada's most rapidly growing areas. Both are surrounded by sensitive ecosystems. Containing the growth of cities and protecting those sensitive ecosystems from urban encroachment have become a critical issue for environmentalists, special interest groups, politicians and the general public. If we are to preserve this planet for our children, and their children, we must come to terms with the facts. We simply cannot continue to sprawl into our vital and precious open spaces.

Smart Growth

Growth is inevitable. In fact, at its present rate it's an unstoppable tsunami. Politicians at all levels, urged on by environmental groups like Green Peace, the Western Wilderness Society, and the powerful Sierra Club, are realizing the importance of protecting the environment from urban sprawl. As we have seen over the past few years, more and more wilderness is being protected for future generations, in the form of parks and green belts. Furthermore, wilderness protection and urban containment are top priorities in many countries around the globe. As politicians wrestle with issues of environmental preservation, the idea of infill housing, as a means of protecting the environment from urban sprawl, has gained unconditional support nationwide.

Ongoing efforts by politicians, social scientists, scholars and urban planners, to deal with the serious issues and effects of urban sprawl, have focused attention on "smart growth". Put simply, this term describes the trend towards re-development of inner cities, suburbs, and small towns, resulting in better use of the land base as well as revitalization of neighbourhoods and economies. It has given rise to new ways of thinking about development and has become the focal point of many debates about where, when, how and for whom development occurs. Smart growth will become synonymous with infill housing. It is the future.

Myths About Infill Housing

There is a very small minority who disagree with infill housing. That has created debates and myths. Listed here are a few of the myths and accompanying realities you should be aware of:

Myth: Infill housing causes traffic congestion.
Reality: On the contrary, people who own infill housing do so because it is close to all amenities. Many prefer walking, cycling or public transportation rather than driving.

Urban Sprawl

Myth: Infill housing strains public services and infrastructure.
Reality: This type of land use makes better use of public services and infrastructure, and therefore it is more cost-effective and cheaper to maintain. Services and infrastructure are already in place and do not necessarily have to be expanded to serve a higher population base.

Myth: People who live in infill housing developments won't fit into the neighbourhood.
Reality: People who buy infill housing become a very big part of the neighbourhood like any other home purchasers. They provide stability and have a sense of pride in ownership. Statistically, owners take better care of their property and become more involved in the community than renters or absentee landlords.

Myth: Infill housing reduces property values.
Reality: The opposite is true. New buildings, occupied and well-maintained by homeowners, increase demand and drive up property values.

Myth: Infill housing undermines community character.
Reality: The community is enhanced by the newer homes, designed with an eye to maintaining and revitalizing the character of the neighbourhood. In addition, the increased population density brings new business and provides reinvigoration with continued prosperity to the community.

Myth: Infill housing density increases crime.
Reality: Infill housing reduces crime. Infill homeowners have a vested interest in keeping

their neighbourhoods crime free, safe and prosperous.

The Facts About Infill Housing

Infill housing has a very positive effect on a community. Here are some facts. Infill housing:

- protects the environment from urban sprawl
- provides a new tax base for the community
  - more housing provides more taxes
- provides jobs in the community
  - each newly constructed home provides 2 years, or 2,000 man hours of employment
- stimulates the economy
  - new consumers in the neighbourhood spend money on goods and services in the community resulting in more residual jobs being created
- provides more affordable housing
  - from secondary suites to new building lots
- leads to opportunities for wealth creation
  - providing financial independence for those who invest in it

To stay current and informed on leading edge "Smart Growth" and infill housing initiatives in North America visit www.smartgrowth.com.

Chapter 3

Real Estate Overview

Chapter 3
Real Estate Overview

Residential property has always been and will continue to be a solid foundation for the creation of wealth. The underlying principles of buying and selling real estate are relatively easy to understand. But even simple buying and selling has its complexities. If you are serious about becoming an infill developer, specialized knowledge is essential. Before you delve into the specifics, you need to be familiar with the fundamentals. The next few pages provide an overview of real estate property types and why their prices fluctuate.

Six Real Estate Categories

Real estate can be broken into six major categories. Each category is comprised of many types and may overlap into more than one category.

Commercial - usually owned by corporations. It includes buildings and spaces where business other than manufacturing is conducted. Commercial space is often used for medical, law or government offices; warehouses, hotels, malls, retail outlets, banks, gas stations, theaters, stadiums etc.

Industrial - usually owned by corporations and found in specially designated areas of a municipality; comprising factories, plants, tank farms, recycling depots, garbage dumps, generating stations, lumber yards, etc.

Real Estate Overview

Residential - owned by individuals or investors and comprises all dwelling places, including single-family houses, detached strata houses, duplexes, town-houses and condominiums.

Recreational - land developed privately or publicly for recreational enjoyment. This includes cottages, hunting lodges, nature parks, trails and sanctuaries. It may be owned privately, corporately or by government.

Agricultural - land used to grow crops and support livestock. It may be owned privately, corporately or by any level of government. Its use is strictly controlled.

Raw - land that has not been developed, altered or improved in any way.

What Makes Real Estate Values Rise?

There are eight key factors that cause real estate values to rise. Understanding your role in effecting those values is vital to your success as a real estate entrepreneur.

Supply and demand - any time demand outstrips supply of a commodity, the price of that commodity will rise. This is the law of supply and demand. Demand is the key; making urban-core properties so expensive. Conversely, lower demand for small-town properties makes them cheaper. Restricted growth in a given area can also contribute to high demand and consequently higher property values. In British Columbia, the growth in Vancouver and Victoria is restricted by

Hidden Profits In Your Back Yard

mountains and the ocean. In Ontario, Windsor is surrounded by Lake Ontario and Lake Huron. In situations with restrictions like that, infill housing provides a viable solution to the housing demand.

Inflation - in real estate, the increase in value of a property, from the time of its purchase to the time it is sold is affected by the cost of living index.

Cosmetic improvements - improving the look of a house or building can dramatically increase the value. Buying the least attractive house on the best street, then giving it the right kind of tender loving care, can pay big dividends.

Capital improvements - renovations continue to be an excellent way to increase property values, especially in the residential market. It is particularly true when a secondary suite is added to an existing house. The demand for this type of rental accommodation is high in any market.

Increasing income - you can increase income by decreasing expenses. For example: reduce utility costs and do not carry bad debt. Tenants who don't smoke or have pets tend to lower maintenance costs with less wear and tear. You can increase cash flow by maintaining a zero rate of vacancy and buying in areas that command higher rents.

Infrastructure changes - new development in an area can have a positive effect on the housing market, increasing demand for housing where changes have occurred. A newly constructed hospital, for example, will attract hospital employees and the elderly to the area.

Economic conversion - occurs when changes are made in the way a property is used, particularly through rezoning or subdividing. Examples include:

- A hotel converted to a condominium complex
- A vacant lot converted to a parking lot
- Residential property converted to commercial or industrial property or vise versa

Infill housing - higher density land use is created by modifying existing residential real estate to allow more housing stock. Examples include:

- Converting an existing house to accommodate a secondary suite
- Rezoning a property to accommodate a duplex or second lot
- Subdividing a property to accommodate a duplex or second lot

What Makes Real Estate Values Fall?

There are eight key factors that cause property values to fall. Understanding the role you can play in preventing those values from falling is vital to your success as an infill housing developer.

Declining neighbourhoods - absentee landlords and/or a high crime rate will cause property values to fall.

Hidden Profits In Your Back Yard

Infrastructure changes - a new highway designed to bypass small communities can have a devastating effect on local real estate values. Federal government cutbacks that close down military bases in or near small communities will drastically effect local real estate values.

Government controls - restrictive zoning changes, moratoriums on housing starts or stringent building codes requiring major work on older dwellings, will effectively decrease property values. Tests and studies disclosing environmental problems such as soil contamination can also decrease property values.

Economics - a downturn in the economy can have a huge effect on real estate values, particularly where there is a single major employer in a related one-industry town.

Supply and demand - when supply outstrips demand, prices will drop. Over-building and/or contractors failure to study Statistics Canada and CMHC reports on demographics and housing trends can cause an over supply, thereby lowering demand.

Urgency to sell - life events that are emotional rather than rational can cause prices to drop dramatically. This urgency tends to appear where divorce, death, foreclosure, transfer or retirement are involved.

Media negativity - news stories focusing on leaky condos, high crime or low income neighbourhoods create fear and will cause property values to drop.

Deferred maintenance - neglecting to paint, landscape, maintain a yard, replace carpets, upgrade kitchens and bathrooms, and general disrepair will lower value.

Traditional Types of Residential Real Estate Investments

There are other traditional types of residential real estate investments worth mentioning in this chapter. Although these investments worked well in the past, they don't work as well today and don't provide the same returns as infill housing. However, they do make for interesting cocktail party conversation.

Revenue property - has been the most popular investment and the easiest to find. This type of property usually means long hours of hard work for the landlord. It can also be plagued with endless problems and offers little return on investment.

The down-side of revenue property ownership includes:

- Being targeted by CCRA audits
- Tenant damage to rental units
- Landlord and tenant arbitration hearings
- Higher interest rates than residential mortgages
- Late night calls for running taps or broken toilets
- No capital appreciation for many years
- Abnormal wear and tear on the property

- Little or no cash flow for several years due to management fees, maintenance costs and vacancies

Fixer-uppers - another way to buy a job if you don't have one. The reality is the labour involved is traditionally three times more than new construction and they are constantly plagued with cost over-runs. This may be caused by things like removing or replacing old fixtures, floors, walls, siding, windows, roofs and other building materials. Other variables that must be considered are rodent infestation, wood rot or structural damage including fire. The problems could be endless.

Estate sales - only recommended if you enjoy paying full retail price for property; unless, of course, the property has potential for rezoning or subdividing which the seller hasn't realized.

Foreclosures - a great way to buy someone else's problem. They are often burdened with liens and debt or in need of structural or cosmetic repair. They should be avoided unless the property has potential for rezoning or subdividing which the seller hasn't realized.

Spec Homes - another avenue many investors have taken with the allure of huge profits. The labour costs are lower than fixer uppers but with the high cost of land acquisition and hefty building loans, these projects rarely see a profit particularly for the inexperienced investor.

Chapter 4

Become
An Expert

Chapter 4
Become An Expert

To be successful as an infill developer you'll need specialized knowledge. You must acquire an instinct for the mechanics and dynamics of the infill housing business; including the many aspects of buying, selling, and financing projects. You'll find it helpful to have appropriate reference materials at your fingertips.

You should start a **personal real estate library** that includes:

- ***Buying Real Estate*** and ***Being Your Own Home Contractor***, both from the Self Council series
- ***Forget About Location, Location, Location***, by Ozzie Jurock
- ***The Roaring 2000s***, by Harry S. Dent, Jr.

If these books are not available from your local bookstore, order them. They are full of valuable tips and information.

Essential references you will need from your **local municipal hall** are:

- A current **municipal zoning map**
- A current **zoning bylaw regulation handbook**
- A copy of the current municipal zoning, subdividing and building **permit procedures**

Become An Expert

You should access a realtor's MLS (Multiple Listing Service) on-line database. This will keep you up-to-date on real estate activities in your area.

CMHC (Canadian Mortgage and Housing Corporation) reports are also an important source of vital information which include:

- Local quarterly **Rental Market** report
- Local quarterly **Housing Now** report
- Local quarterly **Housing Market Outlook** report

Contact CMHC directly for this information. The phone number and address of their offices are listed on their website, www.cmhcschl.gc.ca/cmhc.htm.

From Statistics Canada, access:

- Quarterly **Demographics Statistics** catalogue
- Annual **Demographic Statistics** catalogue

These reports are available on their website at www.statcan.ca or at most public libraries.

Bookmark **my website** for your library, www.dhcarter.com. The site features a mortgage centre for tracking the lowest rates in Canada.

Your library is also the best place to keep **phone numbers** for the team of professionals you'll need. But more on that later.

Review the materials you have gathered and keep this book handy for easy reference. Reread it until your knowledge of the subject grows. The understanding you gain now will lay the foundation for building wealth through residential infill development projects in the future.

Acquire Knowledge

Lack of knowledge is a sure fire recipe for failure, no matter what field you're in. The more knowledge you acquire, the more confidence you will have in your own abilities.

Over the next several months, increase your knowledge about the art of infill housing development by information-gathering, reading, research and experience. Create your own library of reference material. You will also need to put together a team of experts which will be discussed in Chapter 5.

In order to gain confidence with your new-found knowledge, you will have to get your feet wet. Attend public hearings and meetings. Get a feel for the local civic process. Talk to people who have already done rezoning and subdivisions or who are presently engaged in the process. Connect with those people at the public hearings and meetings you attend.

Also get copies of the minutes of any public hearings or meetings held over the past six months. There, you will find the names, addresses and phone numbers of people who are going through, or have gone through, the building, rezoning or subdividing process. Don't be shy: give some of them a call. Most people are more than willing to share their knowledge and experience. Not only will you make new friends, you will establish key contacts that may save you a lot of time, money and possibly, grief.

Make acquiring knowledge a daily exercise. Track CMHC reports, and other related publications. Stay current. Study market conditions, sales, prices, activities. Stay focused, courageous and energized.

Conquer Fear

Most people will tell you public speaking is their number one fear. Does the thought of giving a presentation in front of your local mayor, councillors and the public make you feel nervous? If so, have someone else make the presentation for you.

If you have time, take a public speaking course or join a Toastmasters club to overcome the fear of public speaking.

Many people are intimidated by pressure from peers, family and neighbours who, for reasons of their own, may put up roadblocks to your success. You will have to ignore those naysayers and keep your ultimate goal in sight.

I have included a copy of a letter of disapproval sent to me on one of my projects. It is included in Chapter 11 on page 109. Don't let this kind of nonsense or the negative attitude intimidate or stop you. Instead, allow it to motivate you. It motivated me to write this book!

Stay focused on your goals and keep moving forward.

Take Action

You are almost ready to take action. Before you do, you should know the possible obstacles you may encounter in your quest to become a residential infill developer.

With the help of your realtor, your lawyer and the information in this book, you can navigate your way through any of the business-related obstacles you may encounter on the road to success.

What about those personal demons—fear, laziness, family conflict—that plague us all occasionally and can become roadblocks to success? In order to succeed at infill housing development, you will have to face and overcome those demons.

Maintain Discipline And Focus

Once you have conquered fear and acquired a solid knowledge base, you must follow through with your plans. This is particularly important once you have committed yourself to a purchase or to developing a specific property.

There is no time to be distracted by "flavour of the day" mega trends like network marketing, the stock market or a dot.com business venture. The media hype surrounding these trends is more than some people can resist. But resist you must! Stay focused! Very few people are pursuing real estate using the strategies outlined in this book.

To my knowledge, there are no other books offering a step-by-step guide to residential infill developing for the average person. You can expect to find little competition in this lucrative niche market.

It will be the trends of modern living that fuel prosperity. These trends include changes in birth rates, immigration patterns, divorce rates, housing prices, jobs etc. These trends provide a road map to the future. It is you, the infill housing developer, who must provide the discipline and focus in order to benefit from the rewards.

Don't procrastinate. Do the things that must be done today. Act now! Move forward!

Chapter 5

Getting Started

Chapter 5
Getting Started

You don't need a degree in urban land economics to get started in residential infill development. You do need to be ambitious and organized though. You should also be able to listen and take direction from others. That's the key to becoming successful.

Now you need to find a team of professionals including a realtor, lawyer, surveyor, home designer, home inspector, contractor, municipal planner, banker and eventually, an accountant. Those are people whose knowledge in selected areas is greater than your own. You will need to rely on their specialized knowledge and advice, from beginning to end, to help you succeed.

The Realtor

If you're an experienced home buyer, you may already have a knowledgeable realtor you feel comfortable working with. If you are a first time or inexperienced home buyer, finding a professional realtor you like and trust is an important first step.

The realtor you choose must have experience in rezoning, subdividing and building, and be familiar with the areas of the town or city where you plan to do an infill project. Phone several real estate offices and ask to speak with a top producer who has rezoning and subdivision experience. Meet with each realtor. Treat the

Getting Started

meeting like an interview. Explain your game plan and take notes on the realtor's responses. Choose the person you feel the most comfortable with.

Consider the following criteria when choosing a realtor to help you meet your goals:

- Ability to provide reports on past/present activities for sale prices, vacancy rates and rental costs
- Access to the MLS information
- Access to the MLS daily hot sheet
- Helpfulness in finding other professionals such as a lawyer, surveyor, home inspector, contractor or home designer
- Knowledge of how to make offers that protect you
- Helpfulness in the rezoning, subdividing and building process
- Ability to market your newly created infill project

The Lawyer

Your lawyer will ensure you follow the letter of the law. Choose one who has experience with real estate and who is fluent in rezoning and subdividing procedures. Ask other members of your team to give you the name of a lawyer they use. Get several names and again, treat the initial contact like an interview. Ask these questions:

- Is the fee structured to your liking?
- Will the lawyer be accessible by phone?
- Is the lawyer's office conveniently located?
- Can the lawyer do on-line title searches?

The Home Designer

One way to find a good home designer is to inquire at the municipal planning office. Staff can tell you which home designer's plans are most often submitted successfully. You can also ask your lawyer or realtor for recommendations. You don't need an architect for this type of work. Home designers are less expensive and can do an equally professional job.

When you interview home designers, be sure they meet the following criteria:

- Is the designer fluent in the rezoning, subdividing and building process?
- Can the designer fit a quality house on the new lot?
- Does the designer have a comprehensive understanding of building codes?
- Will the home designer be accessible by phone?
- Is their office conveniently located?

The Home Inspector

Ask your realtor to recommend the name of a home inspector. A home inspector will charge a fee, usually around $250. This service is worth the price. A good home inspection will reveal any major defects in the home or any repairs that are needed. The home inspector documents the information in an inspection report. That report can result in a downward adjustment of the asking price, saving you thousands of dollars. A

Getting Started

home inspection provides you with peace of mind as well.

The Surveyor

In today's real estate market, most lenders require a survey of the property you are purchasing. Ask your lawyer, realtor or home designer to recommend a good surveyor.

The surveyor's precision ensures, among other things, that the home and property lines are accurately located and marked. You will rely on those precise measurements to avoid future conflicts with neighbours or municipalities over property boundaries. An example of a "before" and "after" surveyor's site plan is included on pages 44 and 45.

Before you purchase a property, have a surveyor do an initial survey and become familiar with the property. This survey will include:

- House site location
- Elevations
- Easements
- Right-of-ways
- Encroachments
- Set-backs
- Property lines

Upon completion of your project, the surveyor will return to survey the final property again and complete all the appropriate legal work. The official survey will then be registered at the Land Registry or Land Titles Office.

Hidden Profits In Your Back Yard

Surveyor's Site Plan Before

Getting Started

Surveyor's Site Plan After

In the matter of:

Lot *A*   ~~Block~~   Section *53*
Victoria   District   Plan *30422*

Owner: *Carter*
Contractor:
Solicitor:

I have inspected the *existing house + new construction* and hereby certify that the said structure is situate with respect to nearby boundaries as shown on the sketch below. This document is prepared for mortgage purposes only.

............*John Smith*............ B.C.L.S.

Dated this *6th* day of *June, 1991.*

Re-inspected this 1st day of April, 1992.
............*John Smith*............
B.C.L.S.

The Contractor

When it comes to contracting, you have two choices:
- Hire a contractor
- Be a contractor

Hiring a contractor will cost you more but the advantages of dealing with a professional contractor are: the home will be built faster and with fewer headaches. However, if a contractor does not pay the bills associated with building your house, a lien could be placed on your property, even if you have already paid the contractor for the work. That could get messy. Check the contractor's past performance and get references. Make sure the contractor you select has a good reputation.

Being your own contractor will save you money but you'll need to hire a good journeyman carpenter as the lead trade. You might even find a small contractor to sign on in that capacity.

Regardless of the route you pursue, ask your home designer or realtor to recommend a contractor or journeyman carpenter. Meet with those trades people and conduct interviews before making a final decision. A good carpenter or contractor will have experience in renovations, conversions and additions. They should be pleased to give you references. Call the references and check the contractor's work and reliability.

Contracting and building are worthy of a separate book. Before getting started with this stage of your project, purchase the **Layman's**

Getting Started

Guide To Contracting Your Own Home by David Caldwell. It will be a valuable addition to your library.

The Municipal Planner

Although you don't get to choose this person, the good news is a municipal planner is a professional with complete knowledge and understanding of the rezoning, subdivision and building permit processes in the municipality.

Municipal planners are available for consultation at the municipal hall during normal working hours. They are generally happy to answer questions and explain the rezoning, subdividing and building permit process. They can even give you an indication of how your application may be received by the municipal council, the general public and neighbourhood associations.

The Banker

Finding accommodating bankers is the key to successful financing. Talk to several, including the ones you currently deal with. Tell them you are interested in buying a house. Present them with the following scenarios and see what financing they can provide:

- Purchasing a home with a secondary suite
- Purchasing a home with a partner
- Purchasing a home with subdivision potential

Have your banker develop a financial plan and a pre-approved mortgage for you. Choose the banker who offers you the best options. Keep in mind that, "it doesn't hurt to diversify." Developing a working relationship with several bankers is important. The banker who offers you the best mortgage may not be able to help you establish a line of credit. If that's the case, you may decide to have your mortgage at one bank and your line of credit at another. More on financing in Chapter 14.

The Accountant

Taxes are a serious subject and should never be taken lightly. When you have completed your first project, you may need an accountant. Find a reputable, registered Certified General Accountant or Chartered Accountant the same way you found your other professionals. Make some phone calls, meet and ask questions. An accountant's fees are tax deductible in most cases.

Keep in mind, every project you do will have tax implications:

- If you plan your project as a principle residence, the proceeds are tax free
- If you plan your project as an investment, the proceeds are treated as capital gains
- If you plan your project as a business, the proceeds are treated as taxable earnings for a corporation or proprietorship

Chapter 6

Finding Diamonds In The Rough

Chapter 6
Finding Diamonds In The Rough

You're finally ready to set out into your neighbourhood and find those "diamonds in the rough." You will be making practical use of some of the specialized tools you've gathered in your library: the local MLS catalogue or computer printout, zoning maps and a zoning bylaw regulation handbook. You'll also need a calculator as you conduct your searches.

Sit down with your realtor again and ask for guidance on how to read and use the MLS information and computer printouts, in conjunction with zoning maps and the zoning bylaw regulation handbook.

Once you've settled on a likely looking project, do a feasibility study using the **Preliminary Check-List** in Appendix F (page 162) and the **Feasibility Study Worksheet** in Appendix E (page 160). The generic feasibility studies, included at the end of this chapter, will help you through the process. Here are some hypothetical cases to consider.

Three Hypothetical Cases

The key to finding properties that fit your game plan lies in the various tools you have collected. Zoning maps, MLS catalogues and zoning bylaw regulation handbooks contain all the information you require for now. Start your search using simple strategies.

Finding Diamonds In The Rough

Listed here are some examples, using a fictitious MLS information and rezoning map with the **Generic Zoning Bylaw Regulation Chart** from Appendix A (page 154). Refer to the chart as you review the examples.

One Lot Subdivision

According to the Generic Zoning Bylaw Regulation Chart, **RS1 (Residential Single Family)** lot sizes are a minimum 4,306 square feet. In the MLS listing, you find a house on a 9,000 square foot lot. You check the address in the MLS listing with the street address on the zoning maps and discover it is an RS1 zone: a residential single family dwelling. Using basic arithmetic, you make the following calculation: 9,000 ÷ 2 = 4,500. Bingo! You have just discovered a lot with subdivision potential.

Duplex Lot

The Generic Zoning Bylaw Regulation Chart indicates the minimum **RD1 (Residential Duplex)** lot size is 8,073 square feet. In the MLS listing, you find a house on an 8,100 square foot lot. You check the address in the MLS listing with the address on the zoning maps and discover it is in an RS1 zone. Basic arithmetic, 8,100 ÷ 2 = 4,050, reveals this lot is not large enough to subdivide but is large enough for rezoning to an RD1 duplex: 8,100 is greater than 8,073. Bingo! You have just discovered a lot that has rezoning potential.

Dual Neighbour Split Lot

In the Generic Zoning Bylaw Regulation Chart, RS1 lot sizes are a minimum 4,306 square feet. In the MLS listing, you find a house on a

7,200 square foot lot. Checking the address in the MLS listing with the street address on the zoning map, you discover that the lot is an RS1 zone, but it is not large enough to be subdivided or duplexed. You also discover the neighbour's house is built on a 7,200 square foot lot as well. It too is zoned RS1. Between the two houses, there is enough room for a single lot subdivision. Bingo! Basic arithmetic: 7,200 + 7,200 = 14,400 and 14,400 ÷ 3 = 4,800 square feet reveals you have discovered a lot with subdivision potential. You just have to convince the neighbours they can profit from your legwork.

Subdividing a property is less complicated and time consuming than rezoning a property, particularly if it complies with existing zoning regulations. Learning to pick out properties with subdividing and/or rezoning potential is a skill that takes a little practice, as well as imagination, common sense and courage. There are plenty of opportunities out there. Always do your homework and carefully evaluate the risks associated with purchasing the property. Lawyers call this practicing "**due diligence**".

Finding Diamonds In The Rough For Beginners

Working with your realtor and using the MLS catalogue or computer printout, in conjunction with zoning maps, is the best way to find projects. The types of properties you're looking for are already listed for sale. There are plenty of opportunities in the MLS catalogue to keep you busy.

Finding Diamonds In The Rough

Don't limit yourself though. It is a good idea to read the real estate section of the local newspaper and talk to friends. Stay in touch with FSBO (For Sale By Owner) and new listings of other realtors. You will be surprised at the opportunities you'll find. When you see something that catches your eye, phone for the address and drive by the property. Then have a look on the zoning map to see if the property has subdivision potential. If the property does have potential, do your homework and ask your realtor to help close the deal.

Watch Out For Sharks!

Some properties listed for sale are advertised as having "development potential." These properties are usually **overpriced** with no potential. Check with the municipal planner. Inevitably, you will find the vendors have already tried to rezone and/or subdivide the property themselves and have failed. They still want more than market value for the property and will seldom negotiate. These people are motivated by greed. Stay away!

More About Tools

As a beginner in residential infill developing, it's important for you to become familiar with the tools and terminology you'll be using. Here's a short preview:

Hidden Profits In Your Back Yard

Zoning Maps

A zoning map is a to-scale drawing of a municipal plan for a particular area that shows:

- All zoning areas
- All street addresses
- All street names
- All lot dimensions

Zoning maps may not contain all of the information needed about a given property. If this is the case, contact the municipal hall where individual files are kept on every property in the district. The property file should contain an old site plan or survey certificate. Ask the municipal clerk for a copy. This will aid you in your research.

The MLS

Ask your realtor to access the daily hot sheet and the MLS (Multiple Listing Service) regularly. You can access the MLS online through www.mls.ca. The MLS will provide a wealth of information on each house that is for sale, including:

- Street Address
- Legal description
- Asking price
- Listing date
- Zoning designation
- Photograph of house
- Occupied or vacant
- Owner occupied or rental
- Lot size

Zoning Bylaw Regulation Handbook

A copy of the local municipal zoning bylaw regulation handbook is an absolute necessity for your library. Study the regulations contained in this handbook. We'll delve further into zoning requirements in Chapter 12.

Finding Diamonds In The Rough For Experts

Having completed one or two projects, you are now ready to become more aggressive. Statistics have proven the average house sells every five years. In a community with 1,800 homes, that works out to almost one sale per day. So, armed with zoning maps and zoning bylaw regulations, it's time for you to venture into the suburbs and small towns.

Many small towns experienced rapid growth during the 1940's, 50's and 60's. They now hold hidden treasures for you to discover. Many homes constructed during that time had septic tank and septic field sewage systems. A tremendous amount of extra land was required to accommodate those systems. Consequently, houses constructed during that era were built on large lots. New sewage systems no longer require the same land use. That offers land for infill housing opportunities.

Today, most towns have, or are installing, their own community sewage systems. That means homeowners can disconnect from their septic systems leaving the land formerly needed to accommodate the septic field available for new opportunities. Many of those properties offer excellent potential as redevelopment sites. With some research, creativity and due diligence, you

Hidden Profits In Your Back Yard

could reap profits for years developing those properties.

Whatever strategy you develop, it is important to scrutinize potential properties in a specific area. Start declaring yourself. Obtain the addresses of targeted properties from zoning maps. Research owners' names from the municipal tax roll and phone numbers from the telephone book. The rest is easy. Prepare a small calling card like the following example.

HELLO
My name is **John Smith**
My family and I would like to live
in this neighbourhood
and are presently looking for a
home.
If you are interested in selling,
please call me at 000-0000.

Deliver the cards to homes you have targeted and introduce yourself to the homeowners, or drop a card into the mail box and call back at a later date. Follow up with an occasional friendly phone call expressing your continued interest.

At some point, due to your sheer persistence and the law of averages, you will get a favourable response and a sale will occur. Homeowners may be happy to negotiate with you directly because they benefit in a number of ways: they get an instant sale at a fair market price. They forego the problems and emotional turmoil associated with listing a home for sale; and they keep some of the $10,000 or so they would have to pay in commissions when listing with a realtor. For you, working directly with the homeowner is a great way to cut red tape and maintain control.

Approach the homeowner about sharing the cost of an appraisal to determine a fair market price for the house. Most institutions require an appraisal for mortgage purposes anyway. Keep in mind that appraisers base their estimate of market value on two things: the **purchase price offered** and/or **comparable real estate** that has recently sold in the same or similar area. Since there is no purchase price, the appraiser will only use the comparison method of appraising and then formulate a conservative appraisal, possibly saving you several thousand dollars. That is why ordering an appraisal before making an offer is an important negotiating tool.

The information in this section provides unlimited opportunities, but should only be used by those who have rezoning and subdividing experience. If you are uncomfortable with negotiating a sale directly, or making cold calls, a realtor willing to focus on this type of investment opportunity can negotiate on your behalf. It may enhance your profits and save you time and money.

The Feasibility Study

Whether you're a beginner or an expert, a feasibility study is a "must-do" for every property you're considering. At this stage your financing is in place and you have a thorough knowledge of:

Hidden Profits In Your Back Yard

Feasibility Study Worksheet
Example 1

Project Description: Side-By-Side Double Lot
Step 1 – Calculate Funds Required to Complete the Purchase

Anticipated Purchase Price	$230,000
Closing Costs	
Conveyancing	$ 600
Insurance	$ 200
Survey	$ 300
Home Inspection	$ 200
Appraisal	
Property Taxes (adjust to date of sale)	$ 600
Environmental Assessment Fees	
Other _____	
Total Closing Costs	$ 1,900
(A) Total Funds Required to Complete the Purchase	$231,900

Step 2 – Determine Source of Funds

1st Mortgage	$ 170,000
2nd Mortgage (Seller Take-Back)	$ 60,000
Your Cash	$ 10,000
Your RRSP (eligibility rules)	$ 25,000
Your Line of Credit	
Your Partner's Cash	
Your Partner's RRSP (eligibility rules)	
Your Partner's Line of Credit	
Cash from Investors	
Other _____	
(B) Total Funds Available	$265,000
(C) Funds Available to Finance Development Costs (B) – (A)	$ 33,100

Step 3 – Estimate Development Costs
Hard Costs

Rezoning Application Fees	$ 500
Subdividing Application Fees	$ 1,500
Demolition, etc.	$ 500
Municipal Upgrades	$ 500
Landscaping	
Construction Costs	$ 1,000
Survey	
Other _____	

Finding Diamonds In The Rough

Feasibility Study Worksheet
Example 1 (continued)

Soft Costs
  Borrowing Costs: Interest and Fees
  Architectural/Engineering Design Fees
  Insurance, Legal, Accounting and
  Administration Expenses
  Other _____
(D) Total Estimated Development Costs $4,000

Step 4 – Estimated Gross Sales
  Estimated resale price of original home $230,000
  Estimated sale price of the new lot $ 95,000
  Estimated sale price of new home
(E) Total Estimated Gross Sales $325,000

Step 5 – Calculate Sales Expenses
  Realtor's commission on resale of
  original home $ 10,000
  Realtor's commission on sale of new lot $ 6,300
  Realtor's commission on sale of new home
  Closing Costs on sale of original home
    Conveyancing
    Insurance
    Property Tax (adjust to date of sale) $ 300
  Closing costs on sale of new lot
    Conveyancing
    Insurance
    Property Tax (adjust to date of sale) $ 200
  Closing costs on sale of new home
    Conveyancing
    Insurance
    Property Tax (adjust to date of sale)
  Other _____
(F) Total Sales Expenses $ 16,800

Step 6 – Calculate the Net Proceeds from Sales
(G) Net Proceeds of Sales (E) – (F) $308,200

Step 7 – Calculate Total Project Cost
  Total Cost of Purchase from (A) $231,900
  Total Development Costs from (D) $ 4,000
  Other _____
(H) Estimated Total Cost of the Project $235,900

Step 8 – Calculate Project Profit (or loss)
(I) Projected Net Profit (Loss) (G)–(H) $ 72,300

Note: GST/HST has not been included. Calculate where applicable.

Hidden Profits In Your Back Yard

Feasibility Study Worksheet Example 2

Project Description: Panhandle Lot
Step 1 – Calculate Funds Required to Complete the Purchase

Anticipated Purchase Price		$210,000
Closing Costs		
Conveyancing	$ 600	
Insurance	$ 200	
Survey	$ 300	
Home Inspection	$ 200	
Appraisal	$ 200	
Property Taxes (adjust to date of sale)	$ 600	
Environmental Assessment Fees		
Other _____		
Total Closing Costs		$ 2,100
(A) Total Funds Required to Complete the Purchase		$212,100

Step 2 – Determine Source of Funds

1st Mortgage	$ 140,000	
2nd Mortgage (Seller Take-Back)		
Your Cash	$ 20,000	
Your RRSP (eligibility rules)	$ 25,000	
Your Line of Credit		
Your Partner's Cash	$ 20,000	
Your Partner's RRSP (eligibility rules)	$ 25,000	
Your Partner's Line of Credit	$ 80,000	
Cash from Investors	$ 60,000	
Other _____		
(B) Total Funds Available		$370,000
(C) Funds Available to Finance Development Costs (B) – (A)		$157,900

Step 3 – Estimate Development Costs

Hard Costs		
Rezoning Application Fees	$ 3,000	
Subdividing Application Fees	$ 500	
Demolition, etc.	$ 500	
Municipal Upgrades	$ 1,000	
Landscaping	$ 500	
Construction Costs	$ 140,000	
Survey		
Other _____		

Finding Diamonds In The Rough

Feasibility Study Worksheet
Example 2 (continued)

Soft Costs
- Borrowing Costs: Interest and Fees — $2,000
- Architectural/Engineering Design Fees — $2,000
- Insurance, Legal, Accounting and Administration Expenses — $300
- Other _____

(D) Total Estimated Development Costs — $149,800

Step 4 – Estimated Gross Sales
- Estimated resale price of original home — $210,000
- Estimated sale price of the new lot
- Estimated sale price of new home — $265,000

(E) Total Estimated Gross Sales — $475,000

Step 5 – Calculate Sales Expenses
- Realtor's commission on resale of original home
- Realtor's commission on sale of new lot
- Realtor's commission on sale of new home
- Closing Costs on sale of original home
    - Conveyancing
    - Insurance
    - Property Tax (adjust to date of sale) — $500
- Closing costs on sale of new lot
    - Conveyancing
    - Insurance
    - Property Tax (adjust to date of sale)
- Closing costs on sale of new home
    - Conveyancing
    - Insurance
    - Property Tax (adjust to date of sale)
- Other _____ — $7,000

(F) Total Sales Expenses — $7,500

Step 6 – Calculate the Net Proceeds from Sales

(G) Net Proceeds of Sales (E) – (F) — $467,500

Step 7 – Calculate Total Project Cost
- Total Cost of Purchase from (A) — $212,100
- Total Development Costs from (D) — $149,800
- Other _____

(H) Estimated Total Cost of the Project — $361,900

Step 8 – Calculate Project Profit (or loss)

(I) Projected Net Profit (Loss) (G)–(H) — $105,600

Note: GST/HST has not been included. Calculate where applicable.

Hidden Profits In Your Back Yard

Feasibility Study Worksheet
Example 3

Project Description: Side-By-Side Duplex
Step 1 – Calculate Funds Required to Complete the Purchase

Anticipated Purchase Price		$200,000
Closing Costs		
Conveyancing	$ 600	
Insurance	$ 200	
Survey	$ 300	
Home Inspection	$ 200	
Appraisal	$ 200	
Property Taxes (adjust to date of sale)	$ 400	
Environmental Assessment Fees		
Other _____		
Total Closing Costs		$ 1,900
(A) Total Funds Required to Complete the Purchase		$201,900

Step 2 – Determine Source of Funds

1st Mortgage	$ 150,000
2nd Mortgage (Seller Take-Back)	$ 30,000
Your Cash	$ 45,000
Your RRSP (eligibility rules)	$ 25,000
Your Line of Credit	
Your Partner's Cash	$ 45,000
Your Partner's RRSP (eligibility rules)	$ 25,000
Your Partner's Line of Credit	
Cash from Investors	
Other _____	$ 20,000
(B) Total Funds Available	$340,000
(C) Funds Available to Finance Development Costs (B) – (A)	$138,100

Step 3 – Estimate Development Costs
Hard Costs

Rezoning Application Fees	$ 3,000
Subdividing Application Fees	$ 500
Demolition, etc.	$ 1,500
Municipal Upgrades	$ 3,000
Landscaping	$ 600
Construction Costs	$ 110,000
Survey	
Other _____	

Finding Diamonds In The Rough

Feasibility Study Worksheet
Example 3 (continued)

Soft Costs
    Borrowing Costs: Interest and Fees $ 2,000
    Architectural/Engineering Design Fees $ 1,500
    Insurance, Legal, Accounting and
    Administration Expenses $ 400
    Other _____
(D) Total Estimated Development Costs $122,500

Step 4 – Estimated Gross Sales
    Estimated resale price of original home $ 190,000
    Estimated sale price of the new lot
    Estimated sale price of new home $ 210,000
(E) Total Estimated Gross Sales $ 400,000

Step 5 – Calculate Sales Expenses
    Realtor's commission on resale of
    original home $ 5,700
    Realtor's commission on sale of new lot $ 6,300
    Realtor's commission on sale of new home
    Closing Costs on sale of original home
        Conveyancing
        Insurance
        Property Tax (adjust to date of sale) $ 200
    Closing costs on sale of new lot
        Conveyancing
        Insurance
        Property Tax (adjust to date of sale)
    Closing costs on sale of new home
        Conveyancing
        Insurance
        Property Tax (adjust to date of sale)
    Other _____
(F) Total Sales Expenses $ 12,200

Step 6 – Calculate the Net Proceeds from Sales
(G) Net Proceeds of Sales (E) – (F) $387,800

Step 7 – Calculate Total Project Cost
    Total Cost of Purchase from (A) $201,900
    Total Development Costs from (D) $122,500
    Other _____
(H) Estimated Total Cost of the Project $324,400

Step 8 – Calculate Project Profit (or loss)
(I) Projected Net Profit (Loss) (G)–(H) $ 63,400

Note: GST/HST has not been included. Calculate where applicable.

Hidden Profits In Your Back Yard

Feasibility Study Worksheet
Example 4

Project Description: Secondary Suite
Step 1 – Calculate Funds Required to Complete the Purchase

Anticipated Purchase Price	$190,000

Closing Costs

Conveyancing	$ 600
Insurance	$ 200
Survey	$ 300
Home Inspection	$ 200
Appraisal	$ 200
Property Taxes (adjust to date of sale)	$ 800
Environmental Assessment Fees	
Other _____	
Total Closing Costs	$ 2,300

(A) Total Funds Required to Complete the Purchase — $192,300

Step 2 – Determine Source of Funds

1st Mortgage	$ 140,000
2nd Mortgage (Seller Take-Back)	$ 30,000
Your Cash	
Your RRSP (eligibility rules)	$ 25,000
Your Line of Credit	$ 10,000
Your Partner's Cash	$ 20,000
Your Partner's RRSP (eligibility rules)	$ 25,000
Your Partner's Line of Credit	$ 10,000
Cash from Investors	
Other _____	

(B) Total Funds Available — $260,000

(C) Funds Available to Finance Development Costs (B) – (A) — $ 67,700

Step 3 – Estimate Development Costs

Hard Costs

Rezoning Application Fees	
Subdividing Application Fees	
Demolition, etc.	
Municipal Upgrades	
Landscaping	$ 20,000
Construction Costs	
Survey	
Other _____	

64

Finding Diamonds In The Rough

Feasibility Study Worksheet
Example 4 (continued)

Soft Costs
  Borrowing Costs: Interest and Fees
  Architectural/Engineering Design Fees $ 1,000
  Insurance, Legal, Accounting and
  Administration Expenses
  Other _____
(D) Total Estimated Development Costs $ 21,000

Step 4 – Estimated Gross Sales
  Estimated resale price of original home $255,000
  Estimated sale price of the new lot
  Estimated sale price of new home
(E) Total Estimated Gross Sales $ 255,000

Step 5 – Calculate Sales Expenses
  Realtor's commission on resale of
  original home
  Realtor's commission on sale of new lot
  Realtor's commission on sale of new home
  Closing Costs on sale of original home
    Conveyancing
    Insurance
    Property Tax (adjust to date of sale) $ 200
  Closing costs on sale of new lot
    Conveyancing
    Insurance
    Property Tax (adjust to date of sale)
  Closing costs on sale of new home
    Conveyancing
    Insurance
    Property Tax (adjust to date of sale)
  Other _____
(F) Total Sales Expenses $ 200

Step 6 – Calculate the Net Proceeds from Sales
(G) Net Proceeds of Sales (E) – (F) $254,800

Step 7 – Calculate Total Project Cost
  Total Cost of Purchase from (A) $ 192,300
  Total Development Costs from (D) $ 21,000
  Other _____
(H) Estimated Total Cost of the Project $213,300

Step 8 – Calculate Project Profit (or loss)
(I) Projected Net Profit (Loss) (G)–(H) $ 41,500

Note: GST/HST has not been included. Calculate where applicable.

- Selling prices of resale homes
- Selling prices of new homes
- Selling prices of building lots
- Building costs for new construction
- Building costs for secondary suites

The rest is just a matter of filling in the blanks and doing the arithmetic. On the previous pages you'll find some generic examples of feasibility studies you can use as a guide. When you are ready to conduct your own feasibility studies, you can use and modify the blank **Feasibility Study Worksheet** in Appendix E (page 160).

Total costs will vary from project to project and from municipality to municipality across Canada. Also, no two projects will ever be the same. Be prepared—you never know when Murphy's Law or Caveat Emptor will come into play. Remember, all the costs must be factored into your feasibility study.

Hidden Profits On Main Street Video

A more detailed explanation of infill housing lot types is available in my home study video "Hidden Profits on Main Street." The easy to follow video and workbook covers all 12 examples mentioned in Chapter 7 and provides a visual explanation of the hypothetical examples in Chapter 6. The video can be purchased from my website, www.dhcarter.com .

Chapter 7

Types Of
Infill Housing
Lots

Chapter 7
Types Of Infill Housing Lots

Now that you're familiar with using MLS information, a zoning map and a zoning bylaw regulation handbook, you're ready to look for an interesting and feasible project. As you become more experienced at spotting the various lot types suited to residential infill development, you will begin to realize that projects are only as limited as the scope of your own creativity and imagination.

In the following pages we will study the twelve property types most common in residential infill developing. Use the **Generic Zoning Bylaw Regulation Chart** in Appendix A (page 154) and the **Generic Zoning Map** in Appendix B (page 155) while reviewing and studying the examples. Note that each of the mapped examples in Appendix B corresponds to one of the lot types identified in this Chapter. These are presented here to stimulate your imagination and provide ideas for your own projects.

Use the local bylaw regulations handbook in your research. Spend some time focusing on corner lots. Corner lots are normally larger than other lots in the surrounding area and may offer some of the best opportunities for infill development projects.

Types Of Infill Housing Lots

A: The Dual Neighbour Corner Lot

Many corner lots with excellent development potential go unnoticed. The strategy entails creating a new lot from the backyard of the corner lot and the lot adjacent to it. This development relies on the cooperation of a creative or entrepreneurial neighbour.

This project required only an application for subdividing because the minimum lot sizes were met through existing zoning.

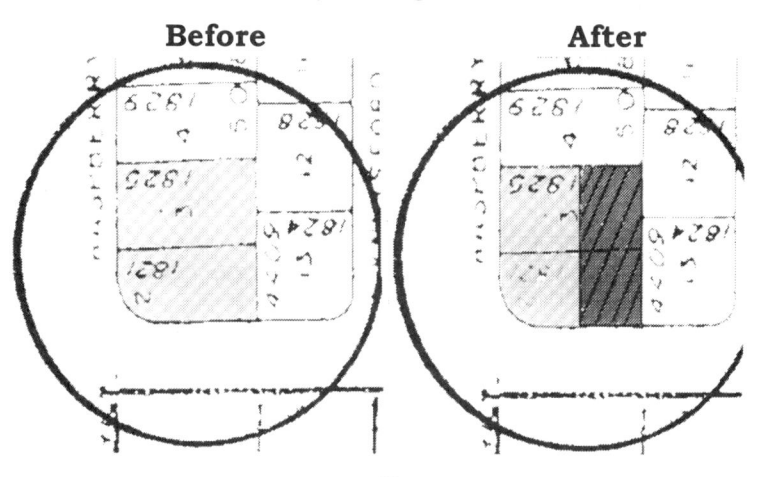

Before   **After**

Hidden Profits In Your Back Yard

B: The Dual Neighbour Split Lot

In this example, a new lot is created using the side yards between two existing homes. As with the corner lot strategy, it relies on the cooperation of a creative neighbour. Some municipalities have designated small lot zones allowing two regular lots to be split into three smaller lots. If this is the case in your area, rezoning may not be required. Your research will dictate the approach you take.

This project required an application for rezoning and subdividing.

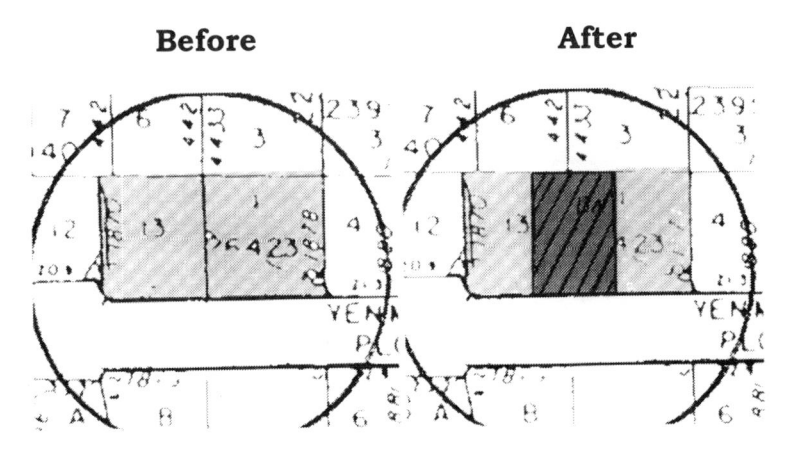

Before   **After**

Types Of Infill Housing Lots

C: The Side-By-Side Strata Duplex Lot

The side-by-side duplex is the best known and most popular development project. It is sometimes called semi-detached housing. In this example, both the existing home and the new unit face the same road frontage; and the two units share a common wall.

This project required an application for rezoning and subdividing.

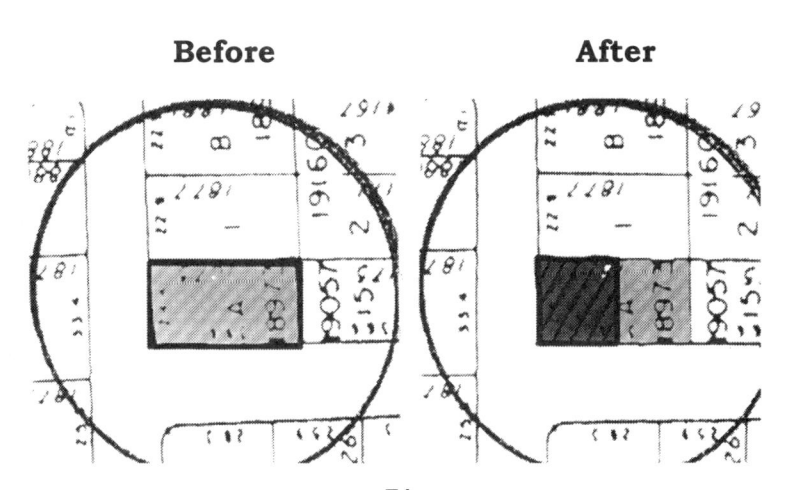

Before   **After**

Hidden Profits In Your Back Yard

D: The Front And Back Strata Duplex Lot

The front and back strata duplex is common in some municipalities but in other municipalities they are not allowed. The front to back development usually requires a large deep lot with a road frontage not wide enough to accommodate a side-by-side duplex or panhandle lot.

This project required an application for rezoning and subdividing.

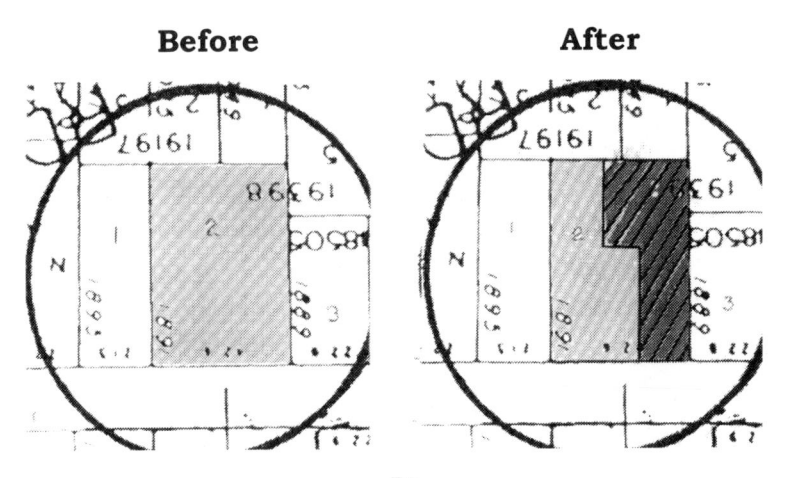

Before   **After**

Types Of Infill Housing Lots

E: The Up And Down Strata Duplex Lot

The popular up and down duplex is commonly found in high density urban municipalities where real estate is at a premium. In this example, a new unit is built by utilizing the attic. The floor of one unit and the ceiling of the other form the common area.

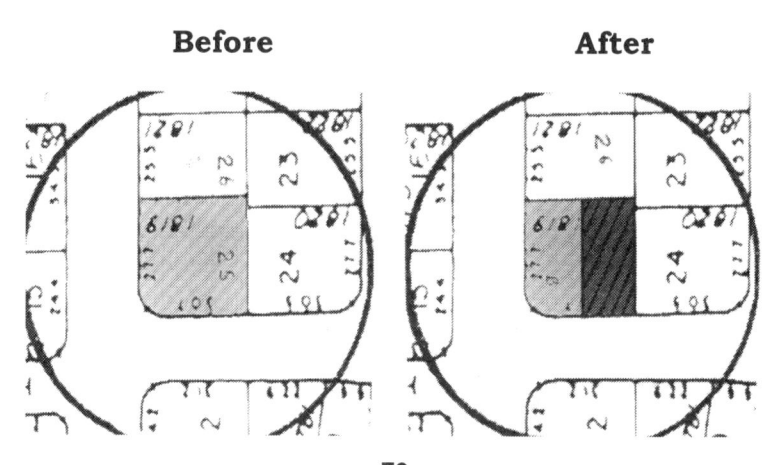

This project required an application for rezoning and subdividing.

Before **After**

Hidden Profits In Your Back Yard

F: The Panhandle Lot

The panhandle works when it is not feasible to subdivide a regular lot because of the minimum width requirements. The new lot is created from the rear yard, with a driveway along one side of the property. Zoning bylaws for this development require the panhandle lot to be larger than a normal lot for safety and fire purposes.

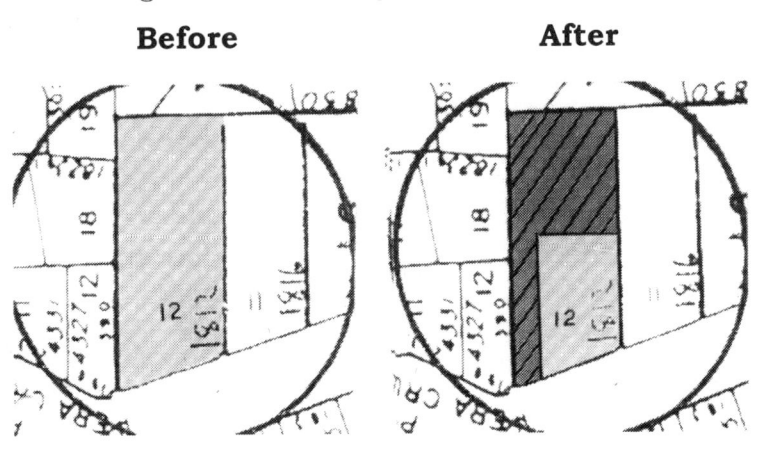

This project required an application for rezoning and subdividing.

Before　　　　　　　　　**After**

Types Of Infill Housing Lots

G: The Dual Neighbour Panhandle Lot, Type 1

Some panhandle developments require creativity and imagination. When the existing lot is not large enough for a panhandle, you can create a larger lot with the cooperation of an entrepreneurial neighbour. Purchasing the land running along the entire length of the neighbour's side yard allows for the zoning requirements to be met.

This project required an application for rezoning and subdividing.

Before   **After**

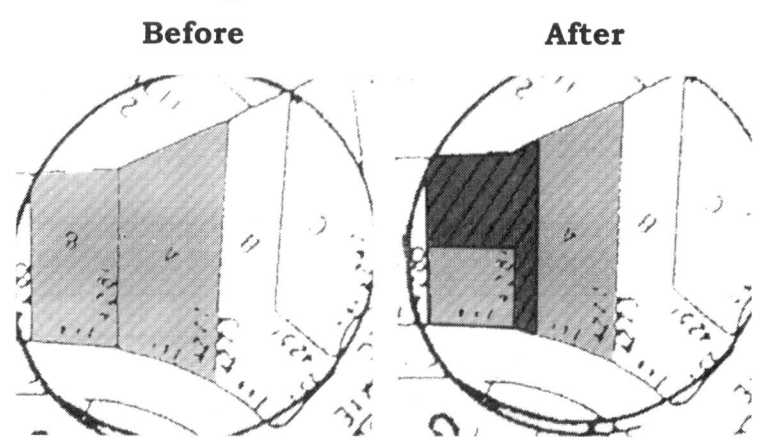

Hidden Profits In Your Back Yard

H: The Dual Neighbour Panhandle Lot, Type 2

This lot was not large enough for a panhandle. With the cooperation of an entrepreneurial neighbour, you could discuss a purchase or joint venture that would utilize the side and rear yards of both properties to be used to meet the zoning requirements.

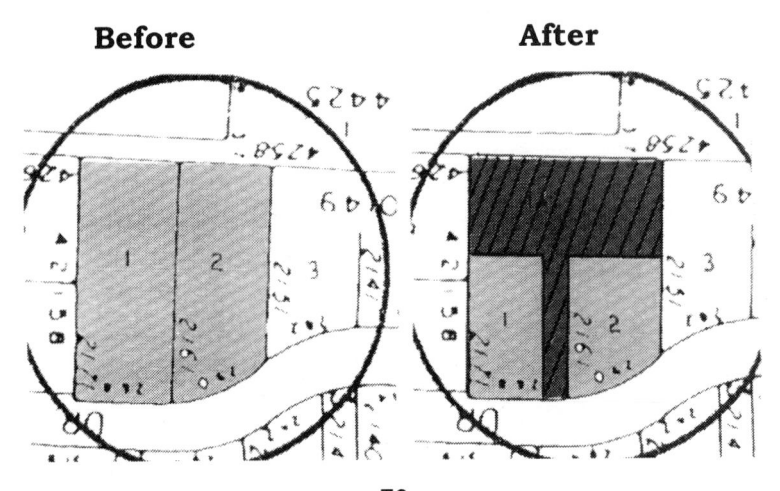

This project required an application for rezoning and subdividing.

Before   **After**

Types Of Infill Housing Lots

I: The Dual Neighbour Panhandle Lot, Type 3

Here again, the existing lot is not large enough for a panhandle. With the cooperation of an entrepreneurial neighbour, a purchase or joint venture would allow the rear yards of both properties to be used to meet the zoning requirements.

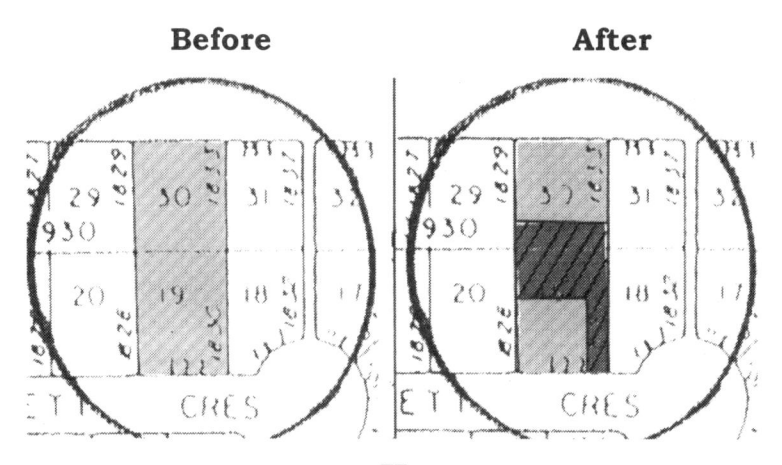

This project required an application for rezoning and subdividing.

Before   **After**

Hidden Profits In Your Back Yard

J: The Side-By-Side Double Lot

The side-by-side double lot can be the most profitable, but is the most difficult to find. Creating the new lot can be as simple as demolishing a garage or as labour intensive and expensive as moving an entire house a few feet. A zoning change is rarely needed and sometimes the property may have two legal titles. Your research will dictate the approach you take.

This project only required an application for subdividing because the minimum lot sizes met zoning requirements.

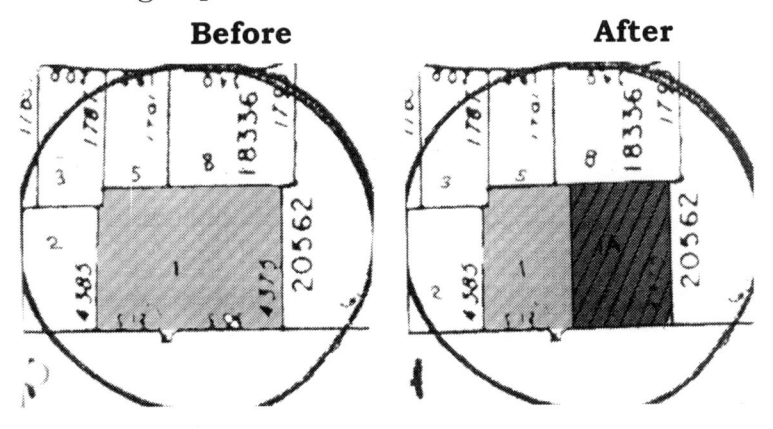

Before   **After**

Types Of Infill Housing Lots

K: The Front And Back Double Lot

The very profitable front and back double lot is difficult to find. The key is a deep lot with road frontage at both the front and rear of the property. If zoning requirements allow, you can create a new lot.

Only an application for subdividing was required here, because the minimum lot sizes met existing zoning requirements.

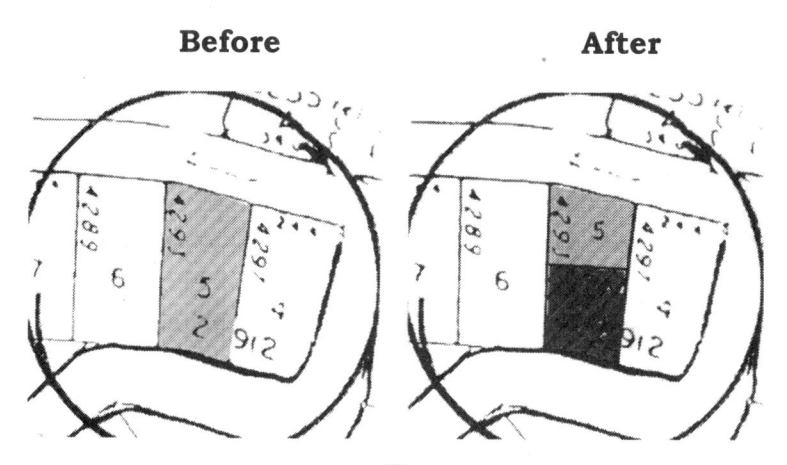

Before   **After**

Hidden Profits In Your Back Yard

L: The Strata Lot

The only difference between this lot and the side-by-side strata duplex lot is the units are totally detached from each other. The units share services and a common area. The units on strata lots can sit side-by-side or face a different road frontage, as in this example. This type of strata development is fairly easy to find and is especially suitable for corner lots.

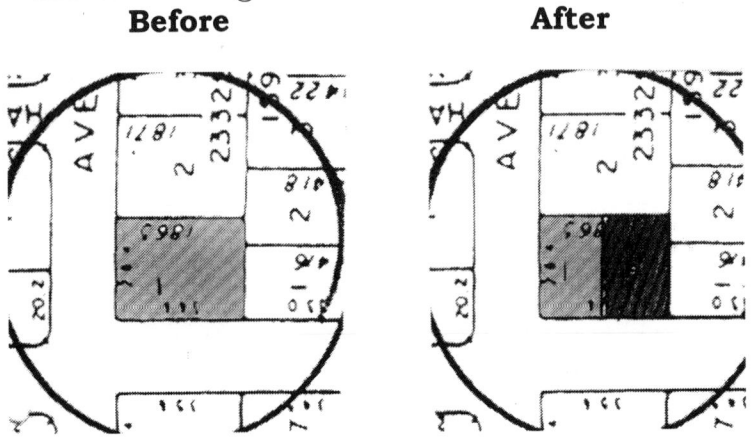

This project required an application for rezoning and subdividing.

Before   **After**

Chapter 8

Secondary Suites

Chapter 8
Secondary Suites

Secondary suites play a key role in the infill housing equation. They provide a very important first step toward increasing cash flow and equity in a house. The cash flow produced by a secondary suite can provide first time home buyers with the financial edge they need to enter the housing market and increase equity.

Secondary suites are legal in some municipalities and illegal or simply ignored in others. Will a secondary suite work for you? You'll have to do your homework. Talk to the municipal planning department for the area you are considering. Inquire about municipal policies and research the local bylaws, resale demands, rental markets and construction costs. Complete a feasibility study before considering any commitment.

Opportunity Knocks

Due to the overwhelming housing crisis in most parts of the country, many municipalities do not make an issue of secondary suites. Frankly, municipalities are often caught between being politically correct, morally responsible and legally liable. However, a legal suite that meets building codes and is properly constructed adds tremendous value to a home. An illegal suite that meets the same building standards adds far less value. This is true even if the cost of creating legal and illegal suites is the same.

Secondary Suites

It would therefore be wise to build a secondary suite only in municipalities where such suites are allowed and encouraged.

The Fundamentals

After doing your research, if you decide to build a secondary suite, keep these points in mind:

- A secondary suite, depending on local interpretation, is generally considered a self-contained living unit in an otherwise single-family dwelling. It is similar to an up-and-down strata duplex but doesn't have the strata zoning and it is not strata titled.
- From start to finish, a secondary suite can be built quickly because there is no time-consuming rezoning process to go through and the existing building structure can be utilized.
- Secondary suites may not need to meet multi-family unit fire codes, but to be on the safe side discuss this with the local authorities to ensure the suite does meet the necessary fire codes. This is a safety and liability issue as well as a resale feature.
- A secondary suite may not need a separate electric meter but it's a good idea to install one anyway for several reasons:
    - it becomes a resale feature
    - it can prevent petty bickering between co-owners, or an owner-occupier and tenant, over the electric bill

- it adds professionalism to the project
- it provides peace of mind

Secondary suites should not be confused with in-law suites. In-law suites are living units which share all of the amenities of the main unit: hydro, common entrances, heat, cable, and phone. Some municipalities allow in-law suites and do not allow secondary suites. Knowing what's legal is important when you are buying, selling or building. Practice due diligence with every house you purchase as rules do change. Before you proceed, find out from your municipal office what policies, rules and regulations apply to secondary and in-law suites.

Great Way To Start

Building a secondary suite or purchasing a home with a secondary suite is a great way for two families, particularly two single-parent families, to enter into the housing market and increase equity quickly. It can also be a great way for a single family to generate extra income.

Building a secondary suite is the most affordable form of housing to produce in Canada because walls, floors and ceilings already exist. Construction costs vary between $20,000 to $40,000 and are fairly consistent from coast to coast (around $25 per sq. ft.). Large fluctuations in cost are usually due to the differences in the number of square feet developed and the quality of finishing. Rental income will vary as well, as it is based on local supply and demand.

Secondary Suites

Be sure to stay current and read the CMHC Rental Market Report and "Suites for Rent" section of your local newspaper. Those resources will provide a clear picture of current rental market conditions.

ROI (Return On Investment)

Investing in a secondary suite in any area of Calgary, Vancouver or Toronto for example, will provide you with at least 342% return on your investment. This percentage is based on construction costs of $35,000 and a monthly rental income of $800 – both very conservative figures. Borrowing $35,000 to construct a suite, with an 8% interest-only, line of credit would cost $2,800 per year for interest payments.

The numbers look like this:

$800 x 12 months = $9,600 (rental income)

$$\frac{\$9,600}{\$2,800} = 342\% \text{ ROI}$$

Can any financial planner offer you this kind of return? The ROI (Return On Investment) will vary, of course, depending on the local rental market conditions and the amount of money you spend constructing the suite. Use the ROI formula when developing your plan:

$$\frac{\underline{\text{Yearly Rental Income}}}{\text{Interest Payments}} = \text{ROI}$$

Types Of Secondary Units

The term "secondary suite" often brings to mind those dark, damp basements with tiny windows and low ceilings – we've all seen them. That doesn't have to be the case anymore. Secondary suites can be built in attics, garages, carports, the first or second floors of a house, etc. In fact, the opportunities are limited only by your own imagination.

More importantly, these suites are a "win win" in todays housing crisis. They provide critical housing that helps protect the environment from urban sprawl. They provide housing in urban centres which encourages people to drive less, walk and cycle more, further protecting the environment from greenhouse gases.

Secondary suites can provide cash-strapped seniors or young families with much-needed supplementary income, and offers urgently needed affordable housing to low income earners. They provide an extremely high rate of return considering the amount of initial investment that is required as clearly demonstrated on the previous page.

Chapter 9

The Opportunity

Chapter 9
The Opportunity

Where are the best places to find the real estate opportunities discussed in this book? Where are those backyards with hidden profits?

Opportunities for backyard profits rarely exist in small town Saskatchewan or New Brunswick, where you can still buy a modest 1,500 square-foot, 3-bedroom resale home for $50,000. Building a new house in those areas would still cost you $150,000. Buying a resale home rather than building a new home in those situations would save you $100,000 in cash or equity.

However, in middle-class, upwardly mobile areas of Toronto or Vancouver, you would be lucky to find a modest home for under $400,000, or a building lot for under $200,000. Why such extremes in pricing? Simply, supply and demand. Anywhere there is a zero or negative population growth, as in Saskatchewan, prices and demand are low. Anywhere there is positive population growth, as in southern Ontario or southwestern British Columbia, prices and demand increase. This is especially evident in areas where population growth exceeds the provincial or national average.

Demographics And Statistics

Humans are creatures of habit and are predictable in both their spending and behavior patterns. Add favourable demographics to the

The Opportunity

equation and you have a recipe for making money in real estate. In his book ***The Roaring 2000s*** (recommended for your library) Harry S. Dent takes an in-depth look at the subject of demographics. According to Dent, demographics directly effect the how, where, when, why, and from whom, you should buy real estate. I agree with his analysis.

Statistics also play an important role in the real estate marketplace. Immigration patterns, migration patterns, births, deaths, the local economy, the local housing market and the local rental market collectively play key roles in the process. All this information is just a click-of-the-mouse or a phone call away. Review the demographic and statistical information contained in the CMHC and Statistics Canada reports mentioned in Chapter 4. Those reports will provide a good indication of the areas to concentrate your research.

The Crystal Ball

Illustrated here is the housing cycle of an average Canadian adult:

- the apartment or suite: 18 to 25 years old
- the starter home: 26 to 33 years old
- the trade up home: 34 to 43 years old
- the vacation home: 44 to 52 years old
- the retirement home: 60 to 70 years old

These statistics, combined with the demographic information in this chapter, paint a clear picture of housing demands at any given time or place, now and in the future.

The Sleeping Giant

While scholars, politicians and society ponder the housing crisis and environmental concerns, no one is focusing on the real issue, the world population explosion. A huge labour void is becoming apparent in North America and by 2015 will be chronic.

Of necessity, the flood gates will open and new immigrants from Asia and Central America will migrate to Canada and the US seeking opportunities. They will be well educated and skilled individuals. Those areas of the globe are just now experiencing their own "baby booms."

Where To Look

Statistics Canada, CMHC and provincial governments have done most of the work for you. All you have to do is capitalize on their efforts. Study the publications relevant to your research: demographic charts, graphs, tables, and information on estimates and projections. You can then produce your own local **LOI's (Leading Opportunity Indicators)** based on that information. Although this research method is far from an exact science, it certainly provides a road map to optimize opportunities in areas that show the most potential.

The Opportunity

Estimates and projections are determined in different ways. Estimates are established using relatively current information gathered through surveys, census, and private and public source documents. Those documents measure every aspect of human life. The statistical information of interest to the infill developer includes deaths, births, migration, immigration, current population, net population growth, housing price increases, and vacancy rates.

Projections are established using relatively current information on emerging demographic trends such as lower birth rates, changing life styles, increase in life expectancy and similar components. These figures are then entered into mathematical formulas to produce objective projections.

The Facts Of Life

In 1800, there were 1 Billion people living on this planet. By 1930, just 130 years later, that number had doubled to 2 Billion people. A mere 44 years later, in 1974, the number had doubled again to 4 Billion. Today, this planet is home to 6 Billion people and the population is expected to double to 12 Billion by the end of this century.

The earth's population is growing at a rate of 1% per year. That means 3 new persons enter the planet every second. Although our birth rate is on the decline in Canada, our net migration is stable at about 150,000 people per year. What does it all mean? It means there is a need, a demand, and indeed a responsibility to provide adequate housing. Infill housing, therefore, is part of the solution to the dilemma of increasing population density.

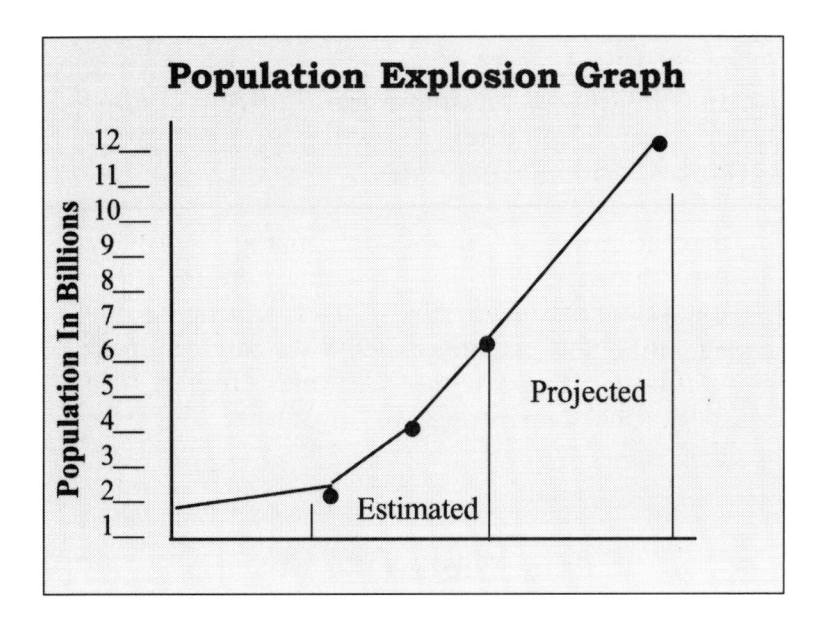

Population Explosion Graph

Population In Billions (1–12), with Estimated and Projected regions shown.

The Changing Household

Households are changing as well. In 1950, the divorce rate was 4% and today, it is 50%. In 1960, the average family consisted of 4 members; by 2000 that number had shrunk to 2.7 members per household.

The number of non-family member households (people living alone or with unrelated persons) will continue to grow more rapidly than households containing family members. The shift from rural to urban lifestyles is another key contributor to the changing demand for housing.

The Opportunity

LOIs (Leading Opportunity Indicators)

LOIs (Leading Opportunity Indicators) provide the science behind the opportunity. The accumulated information provides the infill housing developer with a snapshot of where the greatest hidden potential for infill housing exists, now and in the future. Listed below are the three major LOIs an infill housing developer should be familiar with.

Population Growth
That information is gathered by Statistics Canada, CMHC, provincial governments and the private sector (Royal LePage Quarterly Survey of House Prices). It is then placed in tables that provide valuable analytical information. The major categories that make up total population growth are:

- **Natural growth** - the number of deaths versus the number of births in a given geographical area
- **International migration** - the number of emigrants (landed immigrants) leaving a country versus the number of immigrants entering a country
- **Inter-provincial migration** - the number of people leaving a province versus the number of people entering a province
- **Intra-provincial migration** - the number of people leaving a specific area versus the number of people entering a specific area within the same province

Hidden Profits In Your Back Yard

Real Estate Market

Understanding the real estate market conditions in areas where you will be conducting your research is crucial in making wise and informed decisions. Your local real estate agent will be a huge help. The three areas from the MLS database that can help you formulate decisions, are:

- Local rental prices
- Local housing prices
- Local population growth

The Super Store Index

It is the simplest "no brainer" of the LOIs. Anytime McDonalds, Wal-Mart or Starbucks move into a town, you can be sure the growth within the area is strong. They have more money and time for research than you do. They go where the growth is. All you have to do is follow.

The Canadian National Population Table

The Canadian National Population Table was produced using the information from Statistics Canada's ***Annual Demographic Statistics Catalogue***. To assist your research, I keep a current update on my web site.

As you will note, the Canadian National Population Table clearly demonstrates that Ontario, Alberta and British Columbia are the leaders in the LOI sweep-stakes for overall provincial growth.

The Opportunity

Southern Ontario

Southern Ontario is the powerhouse of Canada. What happens there, socially, monetarily and politically effects the whole country. Toronto is the corporate dynamo at the core. Immigration, a thriving hi-tech sector, bio-medical research and industry, large manufacturing companies, and the head offices of major corporations and financial institutions—all gravitate there to drive the country's economic engine.

It is also cottage country for many Canadians and Americans. Throw in favourable demographics and you have the recipe for a continuing housing explosion!

Research on Southern Ontario should include, but not be limited to, the following cities, towns and their outlying areas: Belleville, Brockville, Chatham, Cornwall, Hamilton, Kitchener, Kingston, London, Oshawa, Ottawa, Peterborough, Richmond Hill, St. Thomas, St. Catharines, Toronto, and Windsor.

Southwestern Alberta

Zero sales tax, a strong economy, corporate head offices and the gateway to the world's largest oil fields are just a few of the reasons migrants from other regions of Canada, and immigrants from countries around the globe, continue to flock to Southwestern Alberta. It is the working person's dream: excellent quality of life, four distinct seasons and the Rocky Mountain wilderness at your doorstep. With a population growth staying well above the national average in many areas, there is a steady demand for housing. Southwestern Alberta provides a golden opportunity for the infill housing developer.

Research should include, but not be limited to: Calgary, Canmore, Didsbury, Edmonton, Red Deer and Sheppard.

Southwestern British Columbia

This region boasts the most moderate climate in Canada and some of the most spectacular scenery in the world. These two facts alone will ensure that it remains the most desirable place to live and retire in Canada. This region also has the highest immigration per capita in the country.

The area can be divided into four distinct regions: the Fraser Valley, the Okanagan Valley, the Sunshine Coast and Vancouver Island. With population growth staying well above the national average together with the move to preserve green space, these areas will continue to provide wonderful opportunities for the infill housing developer.

Research should include, but not be limited to, the following cities, towns and outlying areas: Vernon, Kelowna, Penticton, Summerland, Chilliwack, Mission, Maple Ridge, Port Coquitlam, New Westminster, Burnaby, White Rock, Surrey, Vancouver, North Vancouver, West Vancouver, Richmond, Squamish, Gibsons Landing, Sechelt,

The Opportunity

Victoria, Sooke, Duncan, Ladysmith, Nanaimo, Parksville, Courtenay and Campbell River.

Provincial Statistics

Although British Columbia, Alberta and Ontario are the more obvious regional choices, there are plenty of opportunities in other parts of the country as well. This is where provincial statistics can be used. Any city that shows growth, particularly when it exceeds the national or provincial average, will also present opportunities. The provincial websites listed on page 120 and 121 will be of assistance to those who wish to continue research on other provincial statistics that have not been covered in this chapter.

Sleepers

As you will see from the National Population Table, on my website, Quebec doesn't rate high provincially. However on the Canadian Housing Statistic Table, Montreal rates very well. Although provincially the population growth for Quebec is on the decline, Montreal remains an important international trading centre. It is the birth place of multi-culturalism and is a popular destination for many people migrating to Canada. Projections indicate it will have a healthy infill future.

Another sleeper is Halifax. It continues to show steady growth and is the hub for the Maritimes. It has a deep sea port and is home to the Canadian Navy's Atlantic Fleet. Together with tourism and a healthy maritime spirit, projections indicate that Halifax will have a healthy infill future.

The Canadian Housing Statistics Table

The Canadian Housing Statistics Table was produced using several publications. I will be keeping it updated on my website for your convenience.

Use the blank **Canadian Housing Statistics Table** in Appendix G (page 163) or the one provided on my website, when compiling your own data. Where I have listed several cities across Canada, you can list your own towns or a specific town on a time line using the following past and present quarterly publications:

- Statistics Canada - **Quarterly Demographic Statistics Catalogues**
- CMHC - **Quarterly Housing Report**
- Royal Lepage- **Quarterly Survey Of Canadian House Prices.** This publication can be purchased at any Royal Lepage Office and the cost is minimal. Visit www.royallepage.ca for a list of national offices. I used the single family home type from that publication as the standard when producing the Canadian Housing Statistic Table.

Chapter 10

The Purchase

Chapter 10
The Purchase

On the following pages, I will lay out the steps in making an offer to purchase. You'll also learn how to do a title search and what happens when a deal is closed.

The Offer

Before you make an offer or discuss the price of a house, ask the vendor to order an appraisal and offer to share the cost. This is a starting point. Remember, you are the purchaser, the purchaser is in control and most homes never sell for the asking price. The true value is determined by the price for which the vendor is willing to sell and the buyer is willing to buy. True value is not to be confused with market value. Determining market value is a science and is carried out by an appraiser. When it's time to make the offer, never offer full price—always **negotiate!** Find out why the property is on the market. There may be added incentive to bargain because of:

- divorce or foreclosure
- job transfer
- retirement and a pending move to a smaller house
- major cosmetic repairs needed
- another residence being purchased

Another aspect of the offer to purchase that requires special attention is the **subject to... clauses**. This is where you can stipulate conditions before the deal becomes binding. Including subject to clauses protects you from

The Purchase

unforeseen costs and liabilities. All property purchases could be subject to a:

- Title search
- Home inspection
- Seller take-back mortgage
- Survey
- Lawyer's approval

An offer is a legal document and should not be entered into without the advice of your lawyer. Any major concerns can be addressed by an adjustment of the purchase price or a new offer. Once all the subject to's are addressed or "removed", the offer becomes a binding contract. The offer document can be an **MLS offer to purchase,** if you are using a realtor, or an **offer to purchase form** from a legal kit if you are doing the negotiations yourself. Never make an offer on a property until you check with the municipality to ensure that the property meets all the requirements and regulations that will even-tually come into play with the planned project.

The Title Search

Every real estate sale requires a title search. It must be done before any subject to's are removed. A title search reveals the state of the deed to the property and could include any of the following:

- **Restrictive covenants** – restrictions placed on a property, such as: restrictions to building heights or the protection of endangered plant life
- **Encroachments** – unlawful trespassing on a property, often caused by a building or portion of a building crossing or approaching

the property line
- **Liens** – financial claims by tradespeople, mortgagers, etc. effecting transfer of a property
- **Right-of-ways** – the right to pass over a property freely, according to the nature of the grant
- **Easements** – the right to use property owned by another. This is usually written as an attachment to a deed or can occur through long-term use
- **Mortgage holders** – in order of priority, those to whom an owner has pledged payment of a debt

Conducting a title search is very simple—all you need is the legal description or street address of a property. Have your lawyer do the search or visit the Land Titles or Land Registry Office and ask the clerk to do the search for you. This process is under provincial jurisdiction. The phone number and address of the nearest office is available from your realtor or lawyer. Some Canadian provinces are on the land registry system while others are on the land title system. Each system has its own methodology but the results are the same. Ask the provincial clerk at your local department to explain their system to you.

The Closing

Your lawyer will ensure the statement of adjustments is made and the transfer of title is complete and registered. You are now ready to embark on the process of rezoning, subdividing, building or some combination of the three.

Chapter 11

The Neighbourhood

Chapter 11
The Neighbourhood

For the most part, the rezoning process is designed to be fair to all parties involved. Maintaining a balance between protecting neighbourhood ambiance and staying within the confines of the community plan are key to a successful outcome for the infill developer. Some neighbourhoods/community associations are capable of exerting a huge influence on the way their council considers rezoning decisions. Sometimes there is little or no opposition to a rezoning proposal. At other times, the opposition can be overwhelming. In some neighbours or neighbourhood associations must be consulted before a rezoning application is accepted.

Each municipality is unique. Each neighbourhood association within a municipality is different. Each rezoning application in a municipality is different. Whether it is required or not, neighbours should be consulted out of common courtesy and as a matter of principle. It will also give you an indication of how they feel about infill housing in their area.

In this chapter, we will look at the elements you will need to consider, regarding neighbours and neighbourhoods, before embarking on a development project. The more prepared you are, the better your chances are of getting a favourable response to your plan.

The Neighbourhood

Letter To Neighbours

Once you've found a property you'd like to develop, the next step is to contact the area's neighbourhood association, if one exists. That information is available at the municipal hall.

The neighbourhood association will likely ask you to give a presentation on the development proposal at a community meeting. If there isn't a neighbourhood association, you may need to send a 'letter of intent' to the immediate neighbours within a block or so of your proposed project, and hold a meeting with them. That meeting is sponsored by you and can be held at a local church, hotel or library meeting room. It is held at your expense. The cost should be minimal.

You can expect as many as 50 people to attend, or as few as 2 or 3. You will gain a sense of direction for your project based on the interests and views of the local residents. Some people attending will be in favour of your project and, others may be opposed. Some may attend just to listen to what you have to say before making their decision.

The following is a standard letter I use when conducting my own neighbourhood meetings.

Neighbourhood Meeting For Rezoning Input

The proposed rezoning will convert a single family dwelling to a duplex at: (name or street here). The property is currently zoned RS1, single family. The proposed zoning is RD1, duplex. The property has a total area of 18,400 sq. ft. This allows for a dwelling with a total site coverage of

6,487 sq. ft. I am only seeking a site coverage of 4,039 sq. ft. (Use your own municipal zoning regulations handbook for the applicable square footage and zoning codes).

The new three bedroom home will be professionally designed and built. The existing home will be downsized from a three-bedroom to a two-bedroom with den for my mother. My wife and I live and work locally and have been looking for a home closer to downtown for some time now.

Your input is important to me. I hope you can attend the neighbourhood meeting on (meeting date). The meeting will be held in the Public Library at 123 Burnard Street at 7 pm. If you have any questions about the meeting or the rezoning, please call me at home (home phone number) or email (email address).

At the meeting I will make the following information available:

- Site plan
- Building Plan
- Colour Perspective
- Landscaping Plan

Conducting A Neighbourhood Meeting

Since you are conducting the meeting yourself, arrive early and make sure everything is set up properly. You'll need to provide at least 50 chairs. Make sure there is a chalk board or easle to write on. Bring your realtor or home designer for moral support and to help field questions. Here is a sample format for a neighbourhood meeting:

The Neighbourhood

- Start the meeting on time
- Begin by reading the neighbourhood letter
- Ask these five questions:
  - How can I address your concerns?
  - How would this rezoning effect your property?
  - Can anyone give me reasons why they would not support this rezoning?
  - Can anyone give me reasons why they would support this rezoning?
  - Are there any other concerns or issues you would like to discuss?
- Have those attending the meeting sign a guest book and indicate their support or non-support of the rezoning

Those who support your proposal can be contacted later. You can ask them for a letter in support of the rezoning. This strategy will balance, and quite possibly contradict, any letters addressed to the municipal council that do not support the rezoning.

Most neigbourhood association meetings, or the meetings you conduct yourself, are generally small, usually 10 to 25 people. It is important for you and the local council to receive a general consensus of the neighbourhood views. To be quite honest, the majority of your neighbours will care less. However, it only takes one neighbour to start an anti-development campaign that could have an adverse effect on the project. That is why you need neighbours who support the project. Contacting the municipal clerk, and checking the records for previous rezoning applications in your neighbourhood, is crucial. Any support or disapproval letters will be on file. It will give you a very accurate picture of where the opposition is likely to come from before you start the meeting and also, who may support you and why.

Letters Of Support From Neighbours

There is likely more positive support for your infill project than you think. A carpenter, plumber or electrician living in the neighbourhood may see it as prospective work for themselves or the companies they work for. A neighbour may have a similar property, with development potential as well, and may just be waiting for you to lead the way. That is why neighbourhood meetings are so important.

The following fictional support letter is provided as a guide. Use it to help neighbours who favour of your project, write similar letters to the municipal council, or to be read at a public hearing/meeting in support of your project.

Letter Of Approval For Rezoning
(place rezoning address here)

Dear Members of Council,

I am writing this letter in support of the proposed rezoning at (address here). I attended the neighbourhood meeting held by (your name here) on (date here). I was very impressed with the presentation. The proposed changes to the property fit in very well with our community plan and our neighbourhood.

The Neighbourhood

(Your name here), will be doing a complete renovation of the existing home. This renovation will not only enhance the property but will also increase other property values in our neighbourhood.

The project is environmentally friendly as well. It is part of a "Smart Growth Initiative", where people can work and live close to town without commuting. Less commuting means less pollution. It will also preserve our forest, farms and wet lands from urban sprawl. Projects like this also create jobs in our local economy and form a larger tax base for the community. Every infill house this municipality approves is good for the environment and good for the economy.

Disapproval Letter From A Neighbour

A letter opposing your development project can also occur. I received the following letter for one of my projects. The resentful person was obviously blinded by the $100,000 profit I stood to gain and could not see that the proposed development would provide more housing, create jobs, protect the environment, and improve the neighbourhood. The writer seems to have a full-blown case of the NIMBY (Not In My Back Yard) attitude or maybe the BANANA (Build Absolutely Nothing Anywhere Near Anyone) syndrome. The writer has forgotten or given no thought to the fact that his/her home was likely part of a forest, farm or a wet land habitat 35 years earlier. That is why counter balancing letters of approval from supportive neighbours are so important.

Hidden Profits In Your Back Yard

Mayor and Councillors
Re: Rezoning application for 000 Parklands Drive

Before you is an application to rezone 000 Parklands Drive from the current residential large lot zone to comprehensive development. The owner wishes to construct an additional house near the street and close to the western boundary of the lot.

We have mentioned this intensive development history because the Advisory Planning Committee said while approving this rezoning that Parklands had to accept its share of growth. In our view, Parklands has seen more infill development than any other area of our town and the APC is quite wrong to use this test in making rezoning recommendations.

When Parklands was originally developed approximately 35 years ago, the large lots and narrow streets gave it a unique charm. We are proud of our quiet, peaceful and safe neighbourhood. Even after several years of tremendous growth, it is still a quiet neighbourhood. If the remaining large lots are destroyed through rezoning, we are very concerned that the character of the neighbourhood will be changed forever, and not for the better.

If this developer wants to build new houses, there are hundreds of lots available elsewhere for him to do so. Please do not feel pressured to give this property owner a $100,000 gift of a second lot.

Chapter 12

The Development Process

Chapter 12
The Development Process

It's time to look at the nuts and bolts of the development process. What steps are involved? What should you expect? How long will it take?

The Zoning

Develop a thorough understanding of zoning. Every municipality has its own official plan setting out present and future land use as it relates to its own evolution. That plan determines the location of single-family or multi-family dwellings, schools, hospitals, parks, industrial and commercial areas, as well as water, sewer and other infrastructure services. Study zoning maps to become familiar with the designations used for different types of properties and their current and future uses.

The Zoning Bylaw Regulation Handbook

The Zoning Bylaw Regulation Handbook is the document used by the municipality to regulate land use. The policies found in it are designed to benefit the community, taking into consideration:

- Public health and safety
- Public welfare and growth
- Preservation of amenities and green space
- Conservation of property values
- Future municipal revenues

The Development Process

The bylaws state exactly what land use is permitted. The handbook also provides detailed information on:

Set-backs – the legal distance a building or buildings must be from the front, side and rear property lines
Lot size – minimum requirements
Parking requirements – the number of stalls required for low and high-density housing
Height restrictions – the maximum allowable height a building can be
Uses – to which dwellings may be utilized, such as: in-law suites, secondary suites, boarding houses, home based business, etc.
FAR (Floor Area Ratio) – the inside living dimension, including any additional floors as it relates to the overall square footage of a building
Variances – the process by which zoning bylaws are relaxed. This is usually done when older non-conforming buildings are being redeveloped
Site coverage ratio – the outside dimensions of a building as it relates to the percentage of the lot it covers

The Zoning Bylaw Regulation Handbook is an "absolute must know" for the successful infill developer. The regulations contained in it are legal and strictly enforced. Do not be intimidated by the content; rather, know it and respect it.

The Zoning Bylaw Regulation Chart

Every municipality develops its own zoning codes utilizing an alphabetic and/or numeric combination for each zone (e.g. RS1 - Residential Single Family). A zoning chart is usually included at the front of the municipal Zoning Bylaw Regulation Handbook. Generic zoning code combinations have been used to illustrate zoning examples throughout this book. Although the symbols may change from one municipality to another, the concept remains the same. A ***Generic Zoning Bylaw Regulation Chart*** is in Appendix A (page 154).

The Rezoning Process

Rezoning is the process by which land use is changed. What happens after you submit your application to rezone a property? The mechanics may vary slightly between municipalities, but the process remains more or less the same. There is a preliminary discussion with the municipal planner or office staff, and with neighbours, as covered in Chapter 11. You then submit your application to the municipal planning department, along with an application fee. A file on the property will be prepared and the various departments notified. The file will be forwarded to the engineering department where the supervisor of inspection services will prepare a report on the engineering servicing requirements of the property. A copy of the engineering comments will be forwarded to you.

The municipal planner will prepare a report on the property for the Advisory Planning Committee or similar body. Your application will then be considered by the committee and a recom-

The Development Process

mendation sent to council. Council can decide to reject the application, table it awaiting more information or amendments, or refer it forward through the bylaw process.

If your application is rejected, the municipal clerk will notify you in writing. However, if the council refers it forward, the municipal clerk will prepare a zoning amendment bylaw. Your application will then be placed on an agenda for first and second reading of the bylaw by the council. If approved, a public hearing will be held prior to third and final adoption of the zoning bylaw. An advertisement will be placed in the local newspaper to publicize the hearing and notify residents who live in the area where the property is located. As the applicant, you will also be required to post notice.

The public hearing will be held pursuant to the requirements of the municipal or local government legislation. You will be given the opportunity to present your proposal. Anyone else who cares to speak, either for or against your rezoning, will be heard. Council can then decide to reject or approve the application. If council rejects your application, the municipal clerk will notify you in writing.

If council approves the project, the bylaw is adopted and you will be notified in writing by the municipal clerk.

Refer to the ***Generic Rezoning Flow Chart*** in Appendix C (page 156) for a map of the rezoning process.

The Subdivision Process

Subdividing is the legal process by which a parcel of real estate is divided into two or more separate lots. Each lot has its own legal description and is registered separately with Land Registry or Land Titles. Each new lot can then be bought and sold separately.

Applying for a subdivision is less time-consuming and complicated than rezoning. In most municipalities, there is no requirement for a public hearing. Normally, the only time a complication occurs is when the subdivision does not meet the zoning requirements. Then rezoning and subdivision applications are done concurrently or the application goes before a board of variance.

The general principles involved in subdividing will be more or less the same in every municipality. The process begins with a visit to the local municipal hall and a preliminary discussion with the municipal planner or staff. Once you have made an application and paid the fees, the proposal will be checked out by department staff and a file prepared. Next, the application will go to the various engineering, planning and parks departments for their comments. There will be a site inspection, and then, if applicable, the application will be sent to council for approval. A variance may be required to make the subdivision legal. You may receive approval from council, contingent upon meeting any engineering requirements. Once you have met those requirements, the plan will be approved

The Development Process

and will receive a registration number, new plan number and an address.

Keep in mind, the application may be rejected at any time during the process. Practicing due diligence may help you avoid that scenario. In addition, if the lot is designated as agricultural land or a First Nations burial site, the whole process may involve several more steps.

Refer to the **Generic Subdivision Flow Chart** in Appendix D (page 158) for a map of the subdividing process.

Development Costs

To accurately assess the feasibility of a project, you must carefully consider and calculate all the major development costs. Over-looking or miscalculating any costs could lead to a poor investment. Practice due diligence and use the **Feasibility Study Worksheet** in Appendix E (page 160). Listed here are seven major costs you should consider when determining development expenses:

Demolition - the removal of all or part of a building

Upgrades - the requirement to upgrade water lines, storm drains, sewers, gas lines, electrical services, etc.; upgrades to the existing house, if required

Landscaping - the placement of new trees and shrubs; the removal of old trees and shrubs; installation of sprinklers, retaining walls or fences; removal of or need for more land fill

Lot preparation - rock blasting and excavating required for a driveway or house; removal of, or need for, fill; installation of underground or overhead services

Municipal upgrades - the requirement to install curbs, sidewalks, fire hydrants or street lights that may be a condition of project approval

Financing - borrowing costs, fees and interest payments on mortgages or lines of credit; bonuses to partners or investors

Time - more time spent organizing, planning, scheduling and due diligence ensures faster project completion. Mistakes will be fewer and money may be saved on financing and labour costs. This also enables you to sell or move into your projects sooner

The Building Permit

Once you have created a new lot, whether it is a single, duplex or strata lot, you have new responsibilities. Some municipalities require you to build a dwelling on the newly created lot as a condition of the development process. Regardless of whether you plan to build the house yourself or contract with a builder, the process remains the same. Contact your municipality for details about the building permit process. An application generally requires the following:

- Copies of house plans
- Name and address of homeowner
- Name and address of contractor
- Name and address of home designer
- Survey of site plan

The Development Process

- Colour and building material scheme
- Landscaping plan

Building permits are also required when building a secondary suite.

Canadian Home Builders' Association

The Canadian Home Builders Association is an excellent resource. It provides the infill housing developer with contact information for contractors, current industry news updates, renovation, building and development tips. Here is a list of their websites:

National	www.chba.ca
British Columbia	www.chbabc.org
Alberta	www.ahba.ca
Saskatchewan	www.saskhomebuilders.ca
Manitoba	www.homebuilders.mb.ca
Ontario	www.comeontario.com
Nova Scotia	www.nshba.ns.ca
Newfoundland	www.nfbuilders.com

Strata Title

A strata title gives absolute ownership of a property the same way as fee simple title does. The property can be sold or passed on to heirs. However, strata title means two or more owners share an equal interest in the common areas of the same property such as driveways, party walls,

Hidden Profits In Your Back Yard

roofs, etc. Every province has its own strata title guidelines.

If you are going to specialize in strata duplexing or strata lots, you will need a copy of the applicable provincial government act. Copies of the strata acts for Ontario, Alberta and British Columbia can be obtained from:

Ontario
Toronto
Condominium Act
Publications Ontario
50 Grosvenor Street
Toronto, ON M7A 1N8
Phone: 416-326-5300
Toll Free: 1-800-668-9938
Web Site: www.gov.on.ca

Alberta - Edmonton
Condominium Property Act
Queens Printer Book Store
11510 Kingsway Avenue
Edmonton, AB T5G 2Y5
Phone: 780-427-4952
Email: qp@gov.ab.ca

British Columbia
Victoria
Strata Property Act
Crown Publications
521 Fort Street
Victoria, BC V8W 1E7
Phone 1-888-249-9299
or 250-386-4636
Web Site: www.gov.bc.ca

Alberta - Calgary
Condominium Property Act
Queens Printer Book Store
McDougall Centre,
Calgary, AB T2E 4E8
Phone: 403-297-6251
Email: qp@gov.ab.ca

A word of caution – familiarize yourself with the condominium act but don't be consumed by it. If the process seems complicated, that's because it is. The strata title process should be turned over to a surveyor and lawyer. They can take you through the process.

The Development Process

For a copy of the Condominium Act in each jurisdiction, contact individual provinces through their websites.

Saskatchewan	www.gov.sk.ca
Manitoba	www.gov.mb.ca
Quebec	ww.stat.gouv.qc.ca
New Brunswick	www.gnb.ca
Nova Scotia	www.gov.ns.ca
Prince Edward Island	www.gov.pe.ca
Newfoundland	www.nfstats.gov.nf.ca

The Variables

The long and winding road to prosperity can be as varied as the people who travel it. In fact, some will find it much longer and more winding than others. The length of your journey will depend on a number of variables related to the different aspects of the development process itself. Some of those variables are within your power to control while others are not.

Not within your control, for instance, is the possibility the governing authority, whose good grace you must rely on, will make a change to policies regarding rezoning, subdividing or building, leaving you out in the cold. A moratorium on development in the community can also block progress.

Your application for rezoning, subdividing, or building could be rejected. Maybe the neighbours don't like your proposal and lobby the governing authority against it. Although these situations can exist in a worst case scenario, never underestimate the power of persistence, good luck, past practice and due diligence to propel you forward.

There are many variables in the process you can control. For example, you may run into complications if you miss or reverse steps in the process in which case you simply go back and make the necessary corrections.

Improperly submitted building plans can be rejected and cause you to lose valuable time. Perhaps there is a weakness in your team of experts that can easily be rectified once it is discovered. Remember, neglecting to practice due diligence will only cause you trouble.

When you are rezoning, the process could take about a year from start to finish. However, if you are subdividing, you could get approval in the time it takes to get a building permit, a process that ordinarily takes about a month.

The Product

The end result of all your work will be the product you create, whether it's a strata unit, new home, secondary suite or building lot that enhances your lifestyle or someone else's. More importantly, the effort will have translated into an asset rewarding you with cash or equity and protecting the environment from urban sprawl.

Chapter 13

The Residential Mortgage

Chapter 13
The Residential Mortgage

Residential mortgages play a major role in the infill housing equation. An informed homeowner or investor, who understands the basic concepts and fundamentals of a mortgage, is equipped to make wise financial decisions.

The biggest investment most people will ever make is the purchase of a house. Very few people can afford to pay for a home outright. They need help. Fortunately, the best advice has been advocated by financial freedom gurus for years, the use of OPM (Other People's Money). In this case, using institutional money in the form of a mortgage is a key factor in completing the infill housing formula.

Mortgages come with their own unique built-in financial opportunities. That is why negotiating the interest rate, principle amount, term, frequency of payments and amortization period is as important as negotiating the purchase price of the property. That wonderful leveraging tool called a mortgage can cost you money—or save you money!

Mortgage Definition

The word mortgage is derived from two French words: mort, which means death; and gage, which means pledge. A mortgage is a legal contract registered against a property. The

The Residential Mortgage

mortgaged property provides security to the lender until the loan is repaid. When the loan is repaid, the contract is terminated.

Mortgage Clauses

The institutional mortgage market is very competitive. Although mortgage documents are relatively standard, the clauses included by the different institutions do vary and could affect both your bottom line and your future plans.

Mortgage clauses address some of the finer points of the mortgage agreement. Some or all of them may appear in your mortgage document. So, read the agreement carefully with the guidance of your lawyer, before signing it. Nine major areas covered by mortgage clauses are listed here:

Assumable – when you sell your home the purchaser can assume the mortgage and the document can be transferred into the new owner's name

Non-assumable – the mortgage is due and payable upon the sale of the home

Limited assumability – the purchaser may assume the mortgage with qualifications

Tax account – some lenders require that you pay 1/12 of the property taxes per month, and that the monthly tax amount be blended with the principle and interest payments

Default – failure to pay taxes, insurance, mortgage payments, or keep the property in good repair could activate an acceleration clause causing the mortgage loan to be called. This means the mortgage becomes due and payable immediately and the mortgagee is in a position to initiate legal action against the mortgagor.

Fees – a number of fees may apply. Ensure that you understand exactly what you'll be paying for. Some major costs may include survey, appraisal, mortgage broker, commitment, application or standby fees.

Open mortgage – the mortgage can be paid off at any time during its term, without penalty.

Portable mortgage – the mortgage can be moved from one property to another property, without penalty.

Closed mortgage – the mortgage has a specific contract term. If it is paid off before the end of the term, there is a penalty.

The Key Components Of A Residential Mortgage

Anyone who wants to gain the maximum benefit from a mortgage should understand the components. The seven key components of a residential mortgage are:

Mortgagor – the person who borrows the money
Mortgagee – the person who lends the money, usually a bank or other financial institution
Principle – the loan amount borrowed from the lender
Interest – the amount charged by the lender to the borrower, for use of the money over the term of the mortgage
Term – the length of the mortgage contract. When the term is up, the outstanding balance is due

and payable, or the mortgage is renewed and a new term is negotiated.
Amortization – the length of time, usually measured in years, for the life of a mortgage
Payments – the means by which a loan is repaid. Often payments are a blend of principle and interest calculated over the life of the amortization period.

Canadian Versus American Mortgages

The elements and legalities of a mortgage are the same in both Canada and the United States, although there are some distinct differences. The interest on Canadian institutional money is compounded semi-annually, while the interest on American institutional money is compounded monthly.

American mortgages are normally fully amortized. Canadian mortgages are generally amortized for 20 or 25 year periods, offering terms of 1, 2, 3, 4, 5, 7 and 10 years. In addition, the interest on American residential mortgages is tax deductible while on Canadian mortgages it is not tax deductible.

Interest Rate Comparisons

The following table indicates the relationship between the nominal interest rate, the rate of interest before compounding, and the actual rate

Hidden Profits In Your Back Yard

Nominal Rate	Effective Rate Compounded Semi-annually	Compounded Monthly
3%	3.02%	3.04%
3.25%	3.28%	3.30%
3.5%	3.53%	3.56%
3.75%	3.79%	3.82%
4%	4.04%	4.08%
4.25%	4.30%	4.33%
4.5%	4.55%	4.59%
4.75%	4.81%	4.85%
5%	5.06%	5.12%
5.25%	5.32%	5.38%
5.5%	5.58%	5.64%
5.75%	5.83%	5.90%
6%	6.09%	6.17%
6.25%	6.35%	6.43%
6.5%	6.61%	6.70%
6.75%	6.86%	6.96%
7%	7.12%	7.23%
7.25%	7.38%	7.50%
7.50%	7.64%	7.76%
7.75%	7.90%	8.03%
8%	8.16%	8.30%
8.25%	8.42%	8.57%
8.50%	8.68%	8.84%
8.75%	8.94%	9.10%
9%	9.20%	9.38%
9.25%	9.46%	9.65%
9.50%	9.73%	9.92%
9.75%	9.99%	10.20%
10%	10.25%	10.47%
10.25%	10.51%	10.75%
10.50%	10.78%	11.02%
10.75%	11.04%	11.30%
11%	11.30%	11.57%
11.25%	11.57%	11.84%
11.50%	11.83%	12.13%
11.75%	12.10%	12.40%
12%	12.36%	12.68%

a mortgagor will pay. Not all interest rates are created equal. The more frequent the compounding, the higher the effective rate. Monthly compounding, with its twelve compounding periods annually, will have a higher overall cost than semi-annual compounding, with only two compounding periods annually.

The Interest Rate Comparison Table

The table clearly shows how the frequency of compounding makes a difference in the effective interest rate, especially at higher interest rates.

Most institutions calculate interest semi-annually although some private lenders still calculate on a monthly basis. Before you sign on the dotted line, be sure you know the rate of interest you'll be paying, and how frequently it will be calculated.

The Investment Strategy

In the early 80's, I used every extra dime I had to pay off my home mortgages as quickly as possible. Why? Interest rates were at 15%. Effectively, I was investing in myself at a 15% return on investment by paying off my mortgage quickly.

Times have changed. Today, rather than put extra money into paying down a mortgage, a mortgagor is well advised to invest the extra money in a mutual fund or RRSP. With mortgage rates as low as 4% to 6%, it doesn't make sense to pay off your mortgage quickly nor does it adhere to the mechanics of this book.

Mortgage Books

There are several good books on the market about mortgages. They range from the very complicated to the very simple. I recommend "***Hidden Profits In Your Mortgage***," by Canadian author, Allen Silverstein. Silverstein takes the reader through an easy step-by-step process. The paperback edition is only $15 and is available at most major bookstores.

Overview

Understanding the terms and conditions that apply in the world of residential mortgages is important to the creation of an overall financial plan. Individual lenders will differ from one another in the way they structure mortgage documents. Some may allow weekly or biweekly payment schedules, others may offer balloon payments. Understanding all the options will allow you to obtain the best rates and mortgage for your needs.

Chapter 14

The Financing

Chapter 14
The Financing

Financing is the most important component in any real estate equation. No matter how many great deals you find out there, if you can't afford to buy and hold debt financing then you're not ready to commit to a project. Various financing options are available if you know where to look. They include utilizing mortgage money and RRSPs to finance projects. That type of money is cheap.

The Federal Government has been a big help by providing access to RRSPs and by mandating banks to funnel mortgage money to the residential market. That has encouraged Canadians to become homeowners. It also provides you with an opportunity to capitalize on that generosity and become an infill housing developer. The rule of thumb is KISS (Keep It Super Simple). Residential mortgage money is the cheapest money on the planet and banks love to lend it to participants in the residential market.

Plan A: Residential Mortgage

Residential mortgages are statistically the safest place for banks to invest money. That is why it's important to develop your projects as a homeowner.

Banks have so much money to lend, they are constantly looking for qualified borrowers. Bankers are usually willing to discount their

The Financing

posted rates, particularly for customers who ask. Most Canadians, however, never ask. It seems to be the Canadian way!

Check the interest rates on my website www.dhcarter.com. The Mortgage Centre page will indicate the best rates in Canada. Rates are continually updated.

When you talk to your banker about mortgages, ask two very important questions: "Do you give discounts?" Wait for the answer, then ask, "Is that the best you can do?" Once you have your answer, show your banker the rate sheet from the Mortgage Centre on my website. This strategy may get you an even better rate. Your negotiations with the banker should get you at least a 1% discount. On a $120,000 mortgage, amortized over 25 years, that amounts to a $1,000 savings per year. That's enough money to pay for a survey, insurance, appraisal, home inspection, a great family dinner and this book!

Plan B: Applying For A Mortgage

This is the first step in getting your financial plan in order. Start the process as soon as you finish this book. Get pre-approved so you know how much money you can borrow for a first mortgage.

Banks base their decision on how much they lend using the GDSR (Gross Debt Service Ratio). This insures that mortgage payments and property taxes do not exceed 30% of income. The

Hidden Profits In Your Back Yard

formula is:

> GDSR = (Monthly Income x 30%)
> = Monthly Payments + Property Taxes

For example if your income was $42,000 a year or $3,500 per month, the maximum monthly mortgage payments, including property taxes, you would qualify for are:

> GDSR = $3,500 x 30% = $1,050

Assuming property taxes are $1,800 per year or $150 per month, this provides $1,050 - $150 or $900 per month for mortgage payments (principle and interest). Based on a 3 year mortgage, amortized over 25 years at 6% interest, the $900 would service a $141,000 mortgage. To determine your own mortgage qualifications, use the mortgage calculator available on the mortgage page of my website, www.dhcarter.com.

Banks will only approve up to 75% of the purchase price or appraised value of a property. The only exception is a CMHC high-ratio insured mortgage. However, they don't fit into the infill housing game plan because they are long-term and too expensive.

Banks require three years of income statements to prove you have a track record and the ability to service the debt. If you are self-employed this could prove difficult. Having a partner, friend, investor or father-in-law in on the first project could strengthen your position.

You will need a net worth statement as well. Although it is part of the credit application,

The Financing

presenting a prepared net worth statement when you apply will add credibility and strength to your profile. Below is an example of a net worth statement you can use as a guide.

\multicolumn{3}{c}{**Net Worth Statement** John Doe}		
Item	Assets	Liabilities
Cash	$ 42,000	
RRSP	$ 38,000	
Mutual Fund	$ 6,200	
Rare Stamps	$ 8,200	
Home	$ 210,000	
Car	$ 12,000	
Personal Property	$ 22,000	
Car Loan		$ 3,000
Mortgage		$ 92,000
Visa		$ 3,000
PLC		$ 10,000
Total	$338,400	$ 108,000
Net Worth	$338,400 - $108,000 =	$ 230,400

Special note: Most institutions consider the maximum limits of PLC's and credit cards as liabilities, whether they are paid off or not.

Banks will require proof of a down payment. Establish it with your own cash, RRSP withdrawal, investor, partner or any other creative means at your disposal. Do not give banks any more information than they ask for or require. If you plan to buy property to subdivide or rezone, the banks only need to know the potential. Too much information could wave a red flag and jeopardize your pre-approval.

Bankers are not entrepreneurs. They are trained to deal with the masses and must adhere to very stringent lending guidelines. However, if you plan to buy a house with a secondary suite or plan to build a secondary suite, some or all of the rental income or potential income can be used towards the GDSR. The banker should know your intentions in this regard. Not disclosing that information may make it more difficult to qualify for a pre-approved mortgage or receive a higher mortgage amount.

Plan C: Home Equity

Plan C involves using a home equity line of credit. Most "baby boomers" have paid off their homes or will do so over the next five to ten years, and 80% of seniors over 65 own their homes mortgage free. There are literally Billions of dollars in equity sitting in those homes. Some financial institutions have created "reverse annuity" mortgage schemes in order to profit from equity rich property owners. But smart homeowners aren't biting because of the high risk associated with equity erosion.

Look around you. Many of your family members or friends are living in equity-rich homes. Ask them to become investors in your residential infill development. The home equity they have acquired is doing nothing but collecting dust, when it could be used to benefit both you and them. Get the cash working in the form of an

The Financing

interest-only home equity line of credit. That cash is as important as your pre-approved mortgage. Sign a loan agreement or register a second mortgage on the project to protect the investor's equity. Remember, the interest the investor pays on a home equity line of credit is tax deductible. Give the investor an extra bonus once the development project is finished. Family and friends are better off lending you their home equity than letting it sit doing nothing.

Plan D: PLC (Personal Line Of Credit)

A PLC (Personal Line of Credit) is a financing tool few Canadians consider using. It is similar to a home equity line of credit (in some cases the two can be the same thing) but rather than being secured by a home, it is secured by one or more chattels. They may comprise vehicles, stocks, bonds, mutual funds, GIC's etc. With an interest-only line of credit you pay interest payments only on the outstanding balance—a nice feature. On the downside, when you apply for a mortgage, banks consider the entire amount of your line of credit a liability. Big hint here: you may want to establish your line of credit after you have established a pre-approved mortgage.

Plan E: RRSP (Registered Retirement Savings Plan)

You can use up to $25,000 of your own, or a partner's, RRSP to help you purchase a home. Most Canadians do not understand this financing tool let alone use it. RRSP money used for this purpose is tax free money! This resource is a win-win for everyone involved. A sample of the **Revenue Canada Form** T1036E(99), required to make the RRSP withdrawal under the HB Plan (**Home Buyers Plan**), is included in Appendix H (page 164). Ask your banker or financial planner for further details.

Plan F: Don't Over Extend

Please, never go down the financial food chain by looking through the yellow pages for private lenders, the Federal Development Bank or finance companies. Conventional lending institutions will loan you money based on your assets, debt-service ratio, income and ability to repay. If you apply for funds or a mortgage through a non-conventional lender, you won't be eligible to borrow as much money because they use your financial statement as a weapon against you to extract the highest amount of interest you can afford to service. When the loan or interest-adjustment date is due, the process is repeated with an even higher interest rate. If you are looking for a non-conventional lender, then you haven't done your financing homework, or you're not ready to buy.

The Final Word

The financial resources discussed in this chapter should be considered to make up your purchase, development and construction costs.

Chapter 15

The Sale

Chapter 15
The Sale

Some experts believe real estate prices will remain stable or rise moderately over the next few years. That means there is still a market and a profit in real estate, which is good news for anyone considering the kinds of real estate endeavours discussed in this book. On the other hand, some experts, interpreting trends and demographics, or perhaps using a Ouija Board, predict a melt-down in real estate prices over the next 15 years. So who is more likely to be right about the future of real estate prices—the optimists or the alarmists? No one can predict the market with absolute certainty, but current conditions seem to favour a positive climate for Canada's infill housing market.

Presently, even without considering the massive housing crisis in Canada, there is a huge demand for small, affordable, low maintenance, two or three bedroom homes and suites in "key" areas throughout Canada. Those houses will hold their value. Demographic, immigration and migration patterns all indicate there is no reason to feel anything but optimism for the future.

Turnover

Turnover is a major element of your success as you streamline your game plan and market. You may want to consider two simple strategies to make a project sell faster:

The Sale

- Sell below market value
- Offer a small STB (Seller Take-Back) mortgage to the buyer

And, always leave equity for the next person. Let other people sell emotionally. You sell with this formula in mind:

CASH ➤ ASSETS ➤ PROFIT ➤ REPEAT
Turnover, Turnover, Turnover ...

The following hypothetical example illustrates my point:

You purchase a home valued at $230,000 located on a lot large enough to accommodate a development. An emotionally rigid vendor down the block owns a home of equal value. This unyielding vendor takes a year to sell because he demands his full asking price and won't budge. In the meantime, you re-develop the property and sell the original house for $210,000, discounting it by $20,000. And, you sell the newly created lot for $100,000. So, during the identical time period your equity has increased by $80,000. Who is better off?

The Target Market

You've worked hard to reach the point where you are ready to sell. Who is going to buy the newly created lot and/or house? The market is extensive and covers a wide variety of demographic groups that include:

Hidden Profits In Your Back Yard

Single Parents

In the 1950's the divorce rate was 1 in 24. With today's divorce rate at nearly 1 in 2, single-parent families are driving up the demand for affordable housing. Many single parents need to start their lives over and often have a down payment ready for the right house.

Immigrants

As a country, Canada has much to offer immigrants. We are a developed nation, the largest country in the world, multicultured and leaders in human rights issues. It is no wonder for almost six consecutive years in the 1990's, the United Nations chose Canada as the number one country in the world to live. Hard working immigrants are clamouring to start new lives in this country. They are usually well off, frugal, business professionals seeking modestly priced housing. You can expect this trend, confirmed by Statistics Canada's immigrant numbers, to continue for a long time.

Migrants

There will always be a segment of the Canadian population seeking a fresh start in another area of the country. This predictable migration stimulates local economies and real estate markets in the more desirable locations. Montreal, Toronto, Calgary, Edmonton, Vancouver and Victoria continue to draw people from other regions and this pattern, confirmed by Statistics Canada's report on migration patterns, is expected to remain strong.

The Sale

Baby Boomers

In Canada, "Baby Boomers" are reaching their fiftieth birthdays at the rate of one per minute. Many are "empty-nesters" with large homes they have sold below market value so they can pursue the life style they have dreamed of during their working years: fifth-wheeling, snow-birding, travelling and condominium-living. Eventually, many of them discover all they really want is a small, affordable, maintenance-free home close to all amenities—a home you can effectively provide.

Builders

This market is often overlooked. Small contractors are searching for reasonably priced lots and affordable building projects. They need the projects now and may not have time to go through the development process. Consider doing a joint venture with a builder or selling the entire package to a builder once the rezoning has been completed.

The Pepsi Generation

The "Pepsi Generation" are the "Boomers" who want to have it all, including a second home. Whether they purchase a cottage close to home for weekend getaways or pack up their computers and "snowbird" south to Florida, Arizona and California for the winter, the demand for a second home is exploding and demographically the opportunities are endless. The infill housing developer can supply this market well into the foreseeable future.

Echo Generation

The children of "Baby Boomers" are also a significant target market. Their numbers are as

Hidden Profits In Your Back Yard

big as the Baby Boom generation. They are well educated, environmentally concerned and very receptive to infill housing. Parents of this generation often lend equity from their own homes to allow their children to purchase housing.

Selling Your Projects

Using a realtor to do all the contact, screening and negotiations may be worth the price of the commissions. Or, you could act as your own agent and save the commission costs on each project. This is your decision to make after weighing all the factors. If you choose to be your own sales person, all you need is a "Below Market Value" advertisement in your local newspaper and a "For Sale" sign on your front lawn similar to the illustrations below.

Newspaper Ad

NEWLY RENOVATED
Below Market Value
Seller will carry
ONLY $193,000

OPEN HOUSE
123 Viewcake Road
Sat-Sun 1:00 - 4:00
Phone 000-0000

Lawn Sign

FOR SALE
- Newly Renovated
- Below Market Value
- Seller will carry
- Only $193,000
- View

Call: 000-0000

Statistically, 60% of all homes are sold as a result of a 'FOR SALE" sign on the property.

Chapter 16

The Real Estate Pension Plan

Chapter 16
The Real Estate Pension Plan

As you read this book, you are acquiring knowledge few people possess. You are gaining an understanding of the options in today's real estate market and the benefits of investing in that market. This new knowledge has the potential to propel you to the front of the coming boom in infill housing.

This knowledge can also benefit you in ways we have yet to explore. We can move beyond the tax-free benefits and equity infill housing investment provides, and look at a substantial long-term benefit: the creation of a personal pension plan that can last a lifetime.

How To Get There From Here

The road to financial independence will be an interesting one. Utilizing the ideas and strategies in this book is a good starting point.

Whether you rent or own a house, you can start developing a personal pension plan almost immediately. Familiarize yourself with the infill housing procedures and then just do it.

The Renter

Mortgage rates are so low it has become cheaper to pay a monthly mortgage than to pay

The Real Estate Pension Plan

rent in some areas. Where there are low vacancy rates and high rents, such as Victoria, Vancouver, Calgary, Toronto, Hamilton, Ottawa and Montreal, opportunities for infill housing development are ripe.

The cost of renting a home in those areas ranges from $1,200 to $1,500 per month. Today, payments in that range can support a $250,000 mortgage. By implementing some of the ideas in this book, a renter could leave the rental market and start building home equity. Why throw away money paying off a landlord's mortgage when it's possible to invest in your own future with an infill housing project.

Taking the step from renter to infill developer, will allow you to begin building equity for you and your family.

The Owner

Take a look around. You, or someone you know, may own a property suitable for infill development that has the potential to produce $100,000 in cash or equity. Potential profits in real estate are quite literally hidden by gardens, trees or carports. Discovering them is truly an event. Once the first infill development project is completed, you will have gained the experience to do more projects with increased confidence and success. You will be providing homes for others, protecting the environment and ensuring your own financial independence.

The Five Year Plan

Let's fast forward into the future. Using the strategies set out in this book, let's assume you have completed two projects over the past five years and have just started work on a third project. Your equity has increased by $200,000 and, upon completion of this project, you will gain an additional $100,000 in equity. With clear title on a property worth $300,000, you have now decided to stay in the home. It's proven to be a good deal, working a little smarter in your spare time!

Option 1: Secondary Suite

Let's assume you have also created a three-bedroom secondary suite, in the new home. The secondary suite will provide you with an income of $900 per month (or $10,800 per year) for as long as you stay in the home. There will be tax implications, and you may have the odd vacancy, but overall, it's an excellent investment.

Option 2: Equity Access Investment

You have $300,000 in clear equity in the house. Arrange a mortgage on your home, or a line of credit that you can draw on, for $200,000. Take that money and invest in a solid, top-producing mutual fund or capital investment. Let's assume the rate of return on your investment is 10%. Your annual income will be

The Real Estate Pension Plan

about $20,000. Subtract from that the carrying costs for the line of credit. With an interest rate of 5%, the line of credit will produce approximately $10,000 annually in capital expenses and produce $10,000 in capital growth.

In a 30% tax bracket, the interest costs will produce a tax rebate of approximately:

$$\$10,000 \times 30\% = \$3,000$$

When the dust clears, the investment will produce approximately:

$$\text{Capital Growth} + \text{Rebate} = \text{Net Gain}$$
$$\$10,000 + \$3,000 = \$13,000$$

Ask a financial planner how you can systematically withdraw money from your mutual fund without having to pay taxes. If your financial planner can't explain the details, it's time to get a new planner.

The Bottom Line

Add the $10,800 annual income from the secondary suite and the $13,000 income from your investment. You will have an annual income of $23,800. That is about the same income as a pension plan, accrued from contributions and slaving in the labour force for 35 years. Not a bad deal!

There's more. $300,000 clear title, saves you about $20,000 a year in mortgage payments. Add

Hidden Profits In Your Back Yard

that to the income for a total investment value of $43,800.

Secondary Suite	$10,800
Equity Investment	$13,000
Mortgage Savings	<u>$20,000</u>
Total	$43,800

That is equivalent to having approximately $1,100,000 in a GIC investment earning 4% annually.

There are some homeowners who will consider Option 2, Equity Access Investment, too risky. Utilizing only Option 1 still creates an annual investment value of:

Secondary Suite	$10,800
Mortgage Savings	<u>$20,000</u>
Total	$30,800

That is equivalent to having $770,000 in a GIC investment earning 4% annually.

The Conclusion

I hope the information contained in this book has stimulated your thinking, sparked new ideas and broadened your view of your own future. Getting started is the most difficult step. But, if you stay focused and practice due diligence, you will become a successful, prosperous infill developer.

Opportunities in residential real estate are abundant. There are many people willing to help you along the way. It will take work and courage, but I have no doubt your projects will be fun and exciting.

Happy Hunting! May your wealth grow as you follow the suggestions in this book. Please send me your success stories so I can post them on my website. It will encourage others to follow in your footsteps.

Carpe Diem
Hugh Carter

The Appendix

Appendix A
Generic Zoning Bylaw Regulation Chart

ZONING CODE	MINIMUM LOT DIMENSIONS						MINIMUM SETBACK			SITE COVERAGE RATIO	MAX HGT
	Standard		Panhandle								
	Area	Width	Area	Width	Access		Front	Rear	Side	30% of lot area	
RS1	400 M²	12 M	Not Permitted				6.0 M	9.5 M	1.5 M	120 M²	6.5 M
	4306 sf	39.4 ft.					19.7 ft	31.2 ft	4.9 ft	1291.8 sf	21.0 ft
RS2	460 M²	14 M	Not Permitted				6.0 M	9.5 M	1.5 M	138 M²	7.5 M
	4952 sf	45.9 ft					19.7 ft	31.2 ft	4.9 ft	1485.6 sf	24.6 ft
RS3	560 M²	15 M	835 M²	20 M	6.0 M	6.0 M	9.5 M	1.5 M	168 M²	7.5 M
	6028 sf	49.2 ft	8988 sf	65.6 ft	19.7 ft	19.7 ft	31.2 ft	4.9 ft	1808.4 sf	24.6 ft
RS4	665 M²	18 M	928 M²	23 M	6.0 M	6.0 M	9.5 M	1.5 M	199.5 M²	7.5 M
	7158 sf	59.1 ft	9998 sf	75.5 ft	19.7 ft	19.7 ft	31.2 ft	4.9 ft	2147.4 sf	24.6 ft
RD1	750 M²	20 M	Not Permitted				6.0 M	9.5 M	1.5 M	225 M²	7.5 M
	8073 sf	65.6 ft					19.7 ft	31.2 ft	4.9 ft	2421.9 sf	24.6 ft

The Appendix

Appendix B
Generic Zoning Map

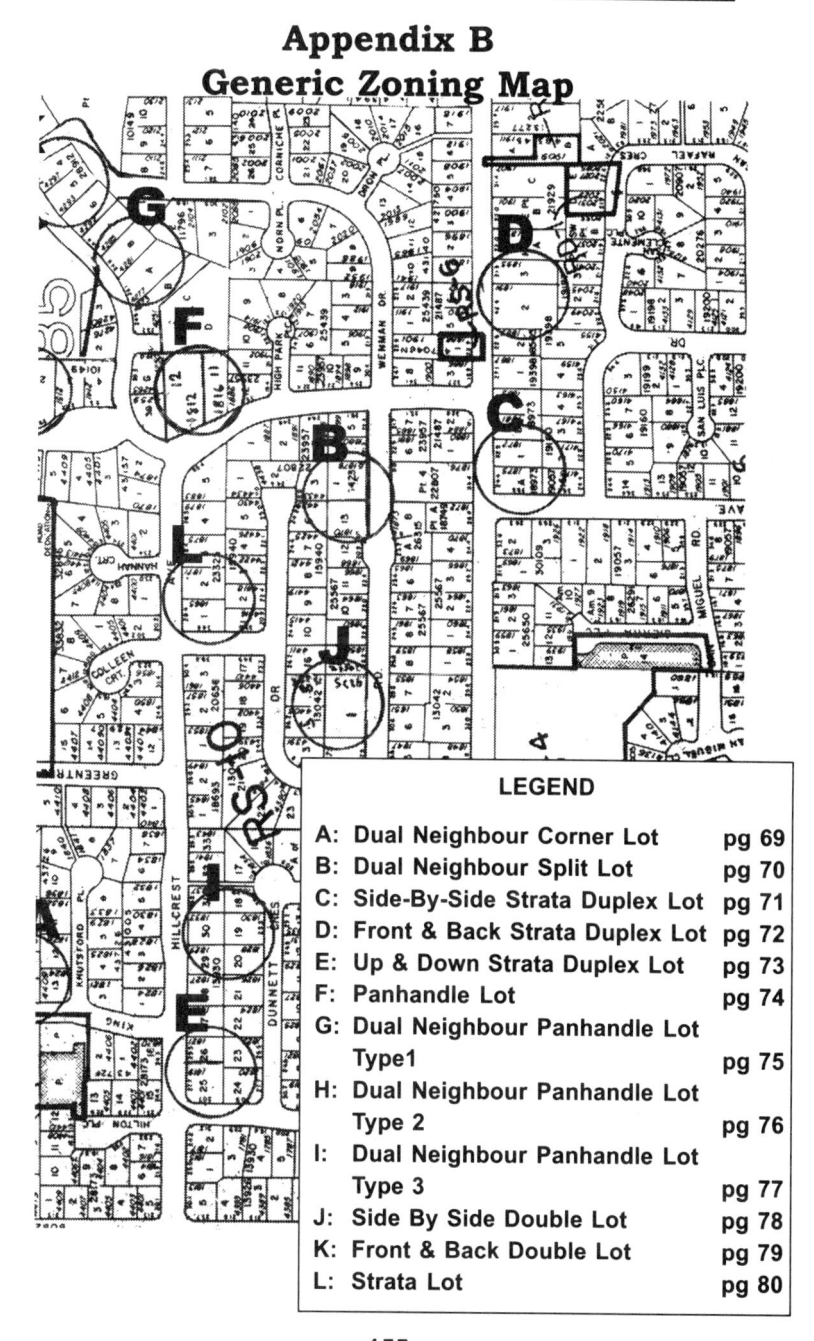

LEGEND

- A: Dual Neighbour Corner Lot — pg 69
- B: Dual Neighbour Split Lot — pg 70
- C: Side-By-Side Strata Duplex Lot — pg 71
- D: Front & Back Strata Duplex Lot — pg 72
- E: Up & Down Strata Duplex Lot — pg 73
- F: Panhandle Lot — pg 74
- G: Dual Neighbour Panhandle Lot Type 1 — pg 75
- H: Dual Neighbour Panhandle Lot Type 2 — pg 76
- I: Dual Neighbour Panhandle Lot Type 3 — pg 77
- J: Side By Side Double Lot — pg 78
- K: Front & Back Double Lot — pg 79
- L: Strata Lot — pg 80

Appendix C
Generic Rezoning Flow Chart

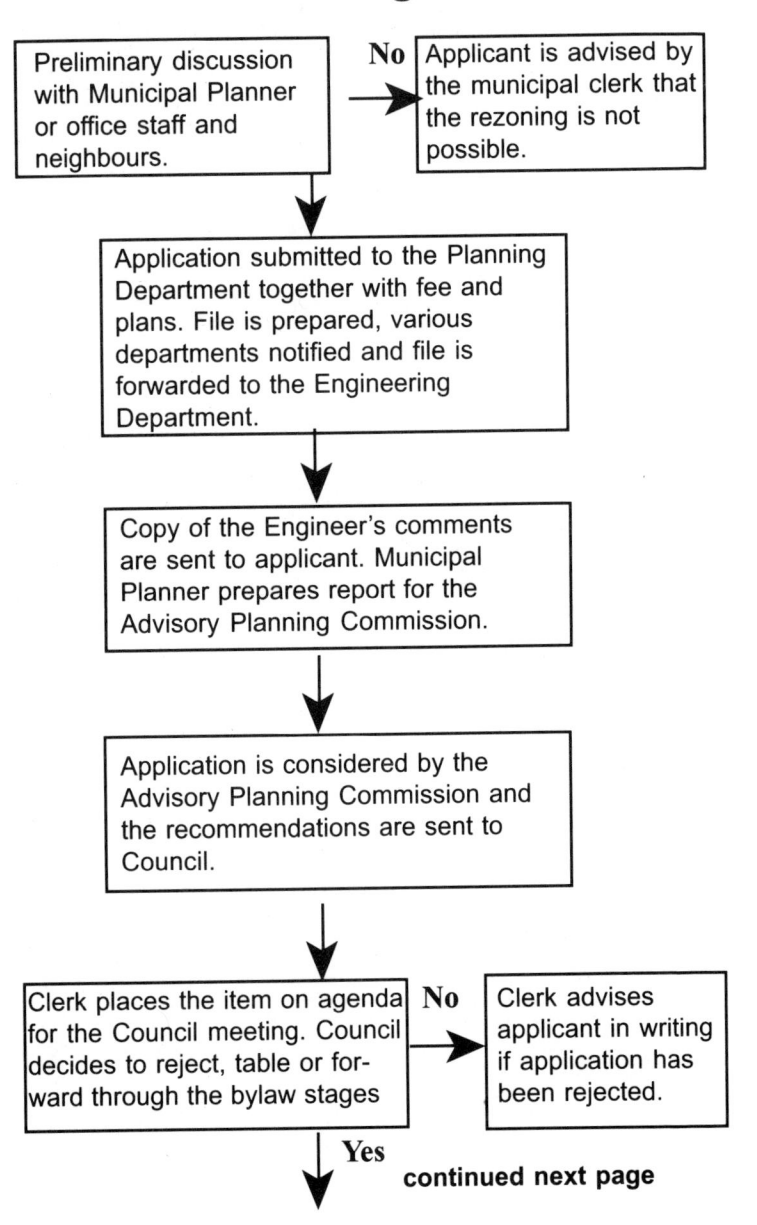

```
┌─────────────────────┐   No   ┌──────────────────────┐
│ Preliminary         │ ─────▶ │ Applicant is advised │
│ discussion with     │        │ by the municipal     │
│ Municipal Planner   │        │ clerk that the       │
│ or office staff and │        │ rezoning is not      │
│ neighbours.         │        │ possible.            │
└─────────────────────┘        └──────────────────────┘
          │
          ▼
```

Application submitted to the Planning Department together with fee and plans. File is prepared, various departments notified and file is forwarded to the Engineering Department.

↓

Copy of the Engineer's comments are sent to applicant. Municipal Planner prepares report for the Advisory Planning Commission.

↓

Application is considered by the Advisory Planning Commission and the recommendations are sent to Council.

↓

Clerk places the item on agenda for the Council meeting. Council decides to reject, table or forward through the bylaw stages. — **No** → Clerk advises applicant in writing if application has been rejected.

↓ **Yes**

continued next page

The Appendix

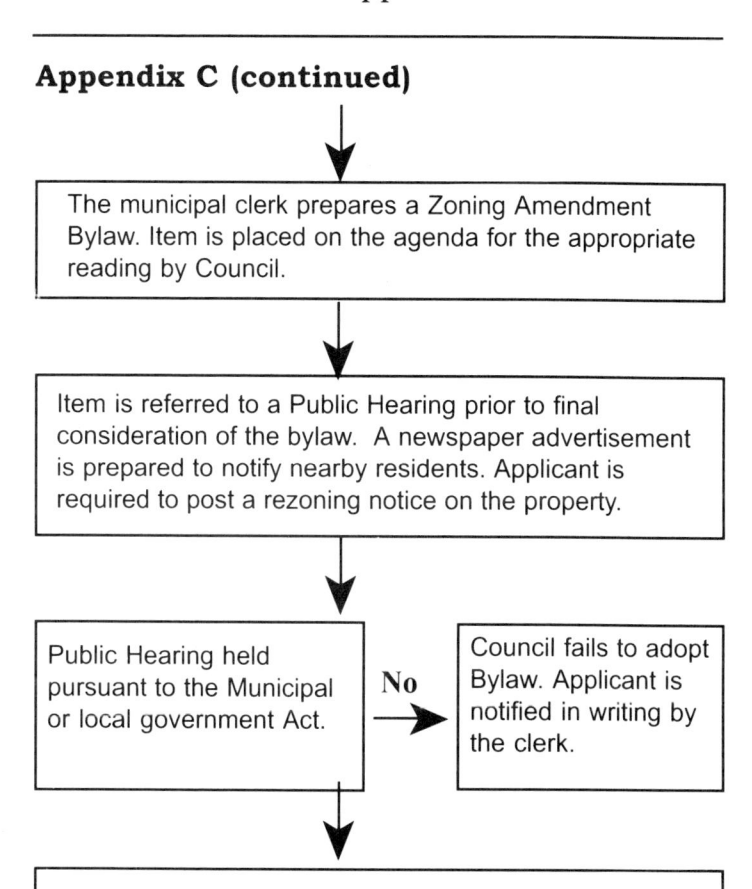

Appendix C (continued)

The municipal clerk prepares a Zoning Amendment Bylaw. Item is placed on the agenda for the appropriate reading by Council.

↓

Item is referred to a Public Hearing prior to final consideration of the bylaw. A newspaper advertisement is prepared to notify nearby residents. Applicant is required to post a rezoning notice on the property.

↓

Public Hearing held pursuant to the Municipal or local government Act. —**No**→ Council fails to adopt Bylaw. Applicant is notified in writing by the clerk.

↓

Council adopts the bylaw amendment. Rezoning is approved. Applicant is notified in writing by the clerk.

Appendix D
Generic Subdivision Flow Chart

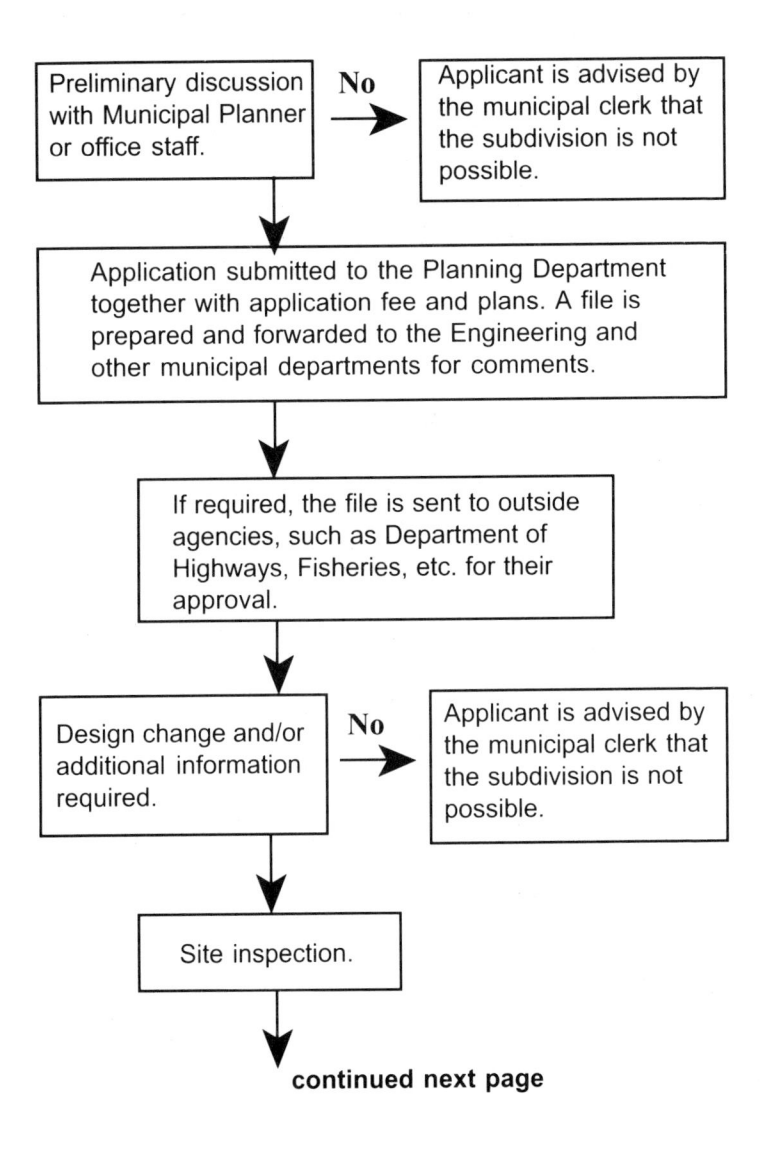

```
┌─────────────────────┐       ┌─────────────────────┐
│ Preliminary         │  No   │ Applicant is advised by │
│ discussion with     │ ────▶ │ the municipal clerk that│
│ Municipal Planner   │       │ the subdivision is not  │
│ or office staff.    │       │ possible.               │
└──────────┬──────────┘       └─────────────────────┘
           │
           ▼
┌─────────────────────────────────────────────────┐
│ Application submitted to the Planning Department │
│ together with application fee and plans. A file  │
│ is prepared and forwarded to the Engineering and │
│ other municipal departments for comments.        │
└──────────────────────┬──────────────────────────┘
                       │
                       ▼
┌─────────────────────────────────────────────────┐
│ If required, the file is sent to outside         │
│ agencies, such as Department of Highways,        │
│ Fisheries, etc. for their approval.              │
└──────────────────────┬──────────────────────────┘
                       │
                       ▼
┌─────────────────────┐       ┌─────────────────────┐
│ Design change and/or│  No   │ Applicant is advised by │
│ additional          │ ────▶ │ the municipal clerk that│
│ information         │       │ the subdivision is not  │
│ required.           │       │ possible.               │
└──────────┬──────────┘       └─────────────────────┘
           │
           ▼
   ┌───────────────┐
   │ Site inspection. │
   └───────┬───────┘
           │
           ▼
   **continued next page**
```

The Appendix

Appendix D (continued)

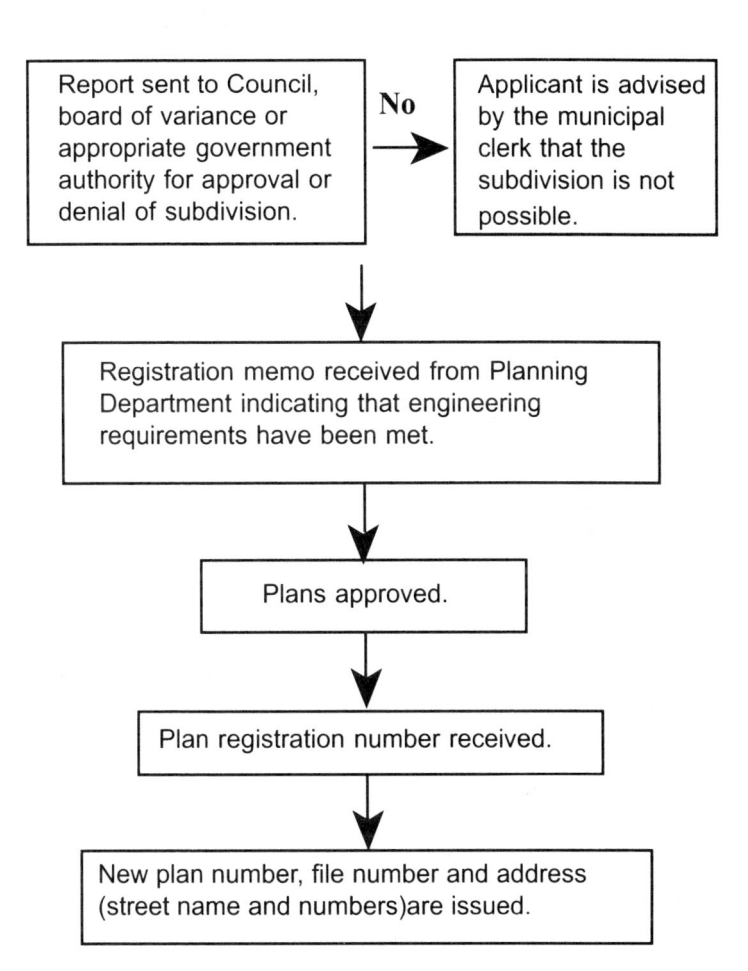

```
┌─────────────────────────┐        ┌─────────────────────────┐
│ Report sent to Council, │   No   │ Applicant is advised    │
│ board of variance or    │ ─────► │ by the municipal        │
│ appropriate government  │        │ clerk that the          │
│ authority for approval  │        │ subdivision is not      │
│ or denial of subdivision.│       │ possible.               │
└─────────────────────────┘        └─────────────────────────┘
            │
            ▼
┌───────────────────────────────────────────────────────────┐
│ Registration memo received from Planning Department       │
│ indicating that engineering requirements have been met.   │
└───────────────────────────────────────────────────────────┘
            │
            ▼
┌───────────────────────────┐
│ Plans approved.           │
└───────────────────────────┘
            │
            ▼
┌───────────────────────────────────┐
│ Plan registration number received.│
└───────────────────────────────────┘
            │
            ▼
┌───────────────────────────────────────────────────┐
│ New plan number, file number and address          │
│ (street name and numbers) are issued.             │
└───────────────────────────────────────────────────┘
```

Appendix E
Feasibility Study Worksheet

Project Description: _____

Step 1 – Calculate Funds Required to Complete the Purchase

Anticipated Purchase Price ☐

  Closing Costs
    Conveyancing ☐
    Insurance ☐
    Survey ☐
    Home Inspection ☐
    Appraisal ☐
Property Taxes (adjust to date of sale) ☐
    Environmental Assessment Fees ☐
    Other _____ ☐
  Total Closing Costs ☐

(A) Total Funds Required to Complete the Purchase ☐

Step 2 – Determine Source of Funds

1st Mortgage ☐
2nd Mortgage (Seller Take-Back) ☐
  Your Cash ☐
  Your RRSP (eligibility rules) ☐
  Your Line of Credit ☐
  Your Partner's Cash ☐
  Your Partner's RRSP (eligibility rules) ☐
  Your Partner's Line of Credit ☐
  Cash from Investors ☐
  Other _____ ☐

(B) Total Funds Available ☐

(C) Funds Available to Finance Development Costs (B) – (A) ☐

Step 3 – Estimate Development Costs

  Hard Costs
  Rezoning Application Fees ☐
  Subdividing Application Fees ☐
  Demolition, etc. ☐
  Municipal Upgrades ☐
  Landscaping ☐
  Construction Costs ☐
  Survey ☐
  Other _____

The Appendix

Appendix E (continued)

Soft Costs
   Borrowing Costs: Interest and Fees
   Architectural/Engineering Design Fees
   Insurance, Legal, Accounting and
   Administration Expenses
   Other _____
(D) Total Estimated Development Costs
Step 4 – Estimated Gross Sales
   Estimated resale price of original home
   Estimated sale price of the new lot
   Estimated sale price of new home
(E) Total Estimated Gross Sales
Step 5 – Calculate Sales Expenses
   Realtor's commission on resale of
   original home
   Realtor's commission on sale of new lot
   Realtor's commission on sale of new home
   Closing Costs on sale of original home
      Conveyancing
      Insurance
      Property Tax (adjust to date of sale)
   Closing costs on sale of new lot
      Conveyancing
      Insurance
      Property Tax (adjust to date of sale)
   Closing costs on sale of new home
      Conveyancing
      Insurance
      Property Tax (adjust to date of sale)
   Other _____
(F) Total Sales Expenses
Step 6 – Calculate the Net Proceeds from Sales
(G) Net Proceeds of Sales (E) – (F)
Step 7 – Calculate Total Project Cost
   Total Cost of Purchase from (A)
   Total Development Costs from (D)
   Other _____
(H) Estimated Total Cost of the Project
Step 8 – Calculate Project Profit (or loss)
(I) Projected Net Profit (Loss) (G)–(H)
Note: GST/HST has not been included. Calculate where applicable.

Appendix F
Preliminary Check-List

	Yes	No
Is your personal real estate reference library in place?	☐	☐
Have you read the suggested books on real estate?	☐	☐
Have you contacted someone who has or is doing a rezoning/subdivision?	☐	☐
Have you attended a public hearing/meeting on rezoning?	☐	☐
Is your team in place?	☐	☐
Realtor	☐	☐
Lawyer	☐	☐
Surveyor	☐	☐
Home Designer	☐	☐
Home Inspector	☐	☐
Contractor	☐	☐
Have you spoken with a Municipal Planner?	☐	☐
Have you submitted the following?		
Application for Rezoning	☐	☐
Application for Subdividing	☐	☐
Application for Building Permit	☐	☐
Have you obtained a pre-approved mortgage?	☐	☐
Do you have financial support from a family member, friend or investor?	☐	☐
Do you have your own extra cash reserve?	☐	☐

The Appendix

Appendix G
Canadian Housing Statistics Table

City (Area)	Population	Net Natural Increase	Net Intern'l Migration	Net Inter Prov.	Net Intra Prov.	Total Growth #	Total Growth %	House Price	Occup Rate	Rent

Hidden Profits In Your Back Yard

Appendix H
Home Buyers Plan Request To Withdraw Funds From An RRSP

Canada Customs and Revenue Agency — Agence des douanes et du revenu du Canada
Revenue Canada — Revenu Canada

HOME BUYERS' PLAN (HBP)
REQUEST TO WITHDRAW FUNDS FROM AN RRSP

Use this form to make a withdrawal from your registered retirement savings plan (RRSP) under the Home Buyers' Plan (HBP). Answer the questions in Part A of Area 1 to determine if you are eligible to make a withdrawal from your RRSP under the HBP. Although some conditions may apply to another person in certain situations, you (the participant) are responsible for making sure that all the conditions are met. For more information, read Chapter 1 of the guide called *Home Buyers' Plan (HBP)*. See the back of this form for information and instructions, or get the guide called *Home Buyers' Plan (HBP)* for more details.

Area 1 – Participant

Part A – Complete the following questionnaire to determine if you can make a withdrawal from your RRSP under the HBP

1. Are you a resident of Canada?
   - Yes ☐ Go to question 2.   No ☐ You cannot make an HBP withdrawal.

2. Has the person who is buying or building a qualifying home entered into a written agreement to do so?
   - Yes ☐ Go to question 3(a).   No ☐ You cannot make an HBP withdrawal.

3(a). Have you ever, before this year, withdrawn funds from your RRSP under the HBP to buy or build a qualifying home?
   - Yes ☐ Go to question 3(b).   No ☐ Go to question 4(a).

3(b). Are you making this withdrawal in January as part of the participation you began last year?
   - Yes ☐ Go to question 4(a).   No ☐ Go to question 3(c).

3(c). Was your HBP balance (see definition on the back of this form) zero on January 1 of this year?
   - Yes ☐ Go to question 4(a).   No ☐ You cannot make an HBP withdrawal.

4(a). Are you a disabled person? (see definition on the back of this form)
   - Yes ☐ Go to question 5.   No ☐ Go to question 4(b).

4(b). Are you withdrawing funds from your RRSP to buy or build a qualifying home for a related disabled person or to help such a person to buy or build a qualifying home?
   - Yes ☐ Go to question 5.   No ☐ Go to question 4(c).

4(c). Are you considered a first-time home buyer (see definition on the back of this form)?
   - Yes ☐ Go to question 5.   No ☐ You cannot make an HBP withdrawal.

5. Does the person who is buying or building a qualifying home intend to occupy the home as their principal place of residence no later than one year after buying or building it?
   - Yes ☐ Go to question 6.   No ☐ You cannot make an HBP withdrawal.

6. Has the person who is buying or building the qualifying home or his or her spouse, owned the home more than 30 days before receiving this withdrawal?
   - Yes ☐ You cannot make an HBP withdrawal.   No ☐ You are eligible (complete Part B).

Part B – Complete this part to make a withdrawal from your RRSP under the HBP

First name and initials _____ Last name _____ Social insurance number (SIN) _____

Address of qualifying home being bought or built (include number, street, rural route, or lot and concession number) _____

City _____ Province _____ Postal code _____ Telephone number ( ) _____

If you are a disabled person (see definition on back), please check this box. ☐

If you answered "Yes" to question 4(b) above, provide the following information about that person:
Person's name _____ Relationship to you _____ Disabled person's SIN _____

Amount of requested withdrawal $ _____   Date of request ▶ Year ____ Month ____ Day ____

Certification
I certify that the information given in Area 1 of this form is correct.
Participant's signature _____

Area 2 – RRSP Issuer

Issuer's name _____   Amount paid (maximum $20,000) $ _____
Issuer's address _____   Plan number of the RRSP from which the withdrawal is made _____

Name and position of person to contact for more information _____   Telephone number ( ) _____   Date of withdrawal ▶ Year ____ Month ____ Day ____

If the participant or the participant's spouse contributed to this RRSP during the 89-day period just before the withdrawal, provide the following information:
Name of contributor _____   Date of contribution ▶ Year ____ Month ____ Day ____

Amount of contribution $ _____   Fair market value of the funds held in this RRSP immediately after the withdrawal $ _____

T1036 E (99)   *Privacy Act* personal information bank number RCT/P-PU005   (Ce formulaire existe en français.)   3150   Canada

Copy 1 – Send this copy to the Pension and RRSP Processing Group, Ottawa Technology Centre, 875 Heron Road, Room 362, Ottawa ON K1A 1A2

The Glossary

Real estate and municipal terminology can be confusing. Be sure to contact your municipality as terms may differ in small but meaningful ways from the definitions offered here. Your municipality's terminology becomes gospel regarding your project.

Appraised Value - the scientific appraisal of a property based on the value of a similar property recently sold in the area.

Assessed Value - the value of a property based on the replacement cost in a given area.

Caveat Emptor - "Buyer Beware." A buyer assumes the risks regarding the condition of a property.

Certificate of Title - acknowledgement that a deed has been registered with the Land Registry or Land Titles department. It contains the legal description and ownership of a property.

Closed Mortgage - a mortgage with a set term which must be honoured until the due date. If early payout is initiated, a penalty is imposed for the discharge.

Conveyance - the transfer of land title from one owner to another.

Deed - a written, sealed instrument of bond contract or transfer.

Hidden Profits In Your Back Yard

Due Diligence - the examination and evaluation of risk a prudent person might be expected to exercise during the course of a transaction.

Easement - the right to use property owned by another. This is usually written as an attachment to a deed but can occur through long-term use.

Economic Conversion - change in value of a piece of land, due to rezoning or subdividing.

Encroachment - unlawful trespassing on another individual's property, often caused by a building or portion of a building crossing or approaching another property line.

Fee Simple - the ownership of land, also called "free hold." The owner has legal possession, power and right to dispose of it in their lifetime or retain it for their heirs.

FAR (Floor Area Ratio) - the inside dimensions of a building including all floor areas.

Infill - creation of small lots within existing land use.

Joint Tenancy - ownership of property by more than one person. If one dies, the other inherits the deed. It is not passed on to heirs.

Land Registry - a provincial department that houses the documents and history of all parcels of land within its jurisdiction.

Land Titles - same as Land Registry.

The Glossary

Legal Description - a full description of property containing lot, plan and parcel identification numbers, as listed in the land titles department; and roll number, as listed in municipal records.

Lien - a claim placed on a property for money owed. It effects the transfer of property.

Lot Line - surveyed delineation of boundaries of a parcel of land.

Market Value - the value of a parcel of land determined by an appraiser taking into consideration condition of property, lot size, improvements, structures, area, services and recent selling prices in the area.

Mortgage - a pledge or security on a particular property for payment of a debt.

Mortgagee - one who lends money.

Mortgagor - one who borrows money using real estate as security.

Municipality - a city, town, urban or suburban area having its own incorporated government. Its powers are exercised by individuals elected by those who live within its boundaries.

Non-Conforming - a building that does not conform to existing bylaws.

Open Mortgage - a mortgage with a set term, which can be paid out before the term date without incurring a penalty.

Hidden Profits In Your Back Yard

Parcel - a lot or block of land in a subdivided area that is assessed singley.

Portable Mortgage - a mortgage that can be moved from property to property without penalty.

Property Line - documented boundaries of a given parcel of land.

Restrictive Covenant - a condition placed on a property. It could restrict building height, plant life or secondary suites.

Rezone - the process by which property is changed from one use to another.

Right-of-Way - the right to pass over another property freely, according to the nature of a grant.

Seller Take-Back Mortgage - a seller provides mortgage financing in order to facilitate the sale of a property.

Setback - the legal distance a building must be from front, side and rear property lines.

Site Coverage Ratio - the outside dimension of a building and the percentage of the lot it covers.

Strata Title - two or more separate titles that share common areas.

Subdivide - to divide property into smaller parcels. Each parcel is registered separately at the Land Registry or Land Titles office.

The Glossary

Survey Pin - an iron peg placed in the ground by a surveyor to indicate property lines.

Survey Stake - a stake placed in the ground by a surveyor to indicate property lines.

Tenants-In-Common - joint ownership of property by two or more people that may be equally or unequally shared. Ownership can be passed to heirs, not to remaining tenants-in-common.

Title - documented ownership of property.

Title Deed - documented proof of legal ownership of property.

Title Search - research to determine the history, state and chain of ownership of a property.

True Value - price a vendor is willing to sell and a purchaser is willing to pay for a property.

Variance - relaxation of zoning bylaw regulations. Often occurs when an older non-conforming building is redeveloped.

Zoning - a specified land use in a specific jurisdiction.

Disclaimer

This book has been designed as a guide only. Every attempt has been made to ensure the content is free of errors and omissions. The author, researchers, advisors and distributors of this information disclaim any liability for loss in connection with the interpretation of content, in whole or in part.

By purchasing this book it is understood you accept this disclaimer and accept full responsibility for your own actions regarding this material. The services of an appropriate competent professional should be sought when legal, accounting, tax, investment, financial planning or other advice is required.

Praise for "Hidden Profits In Your Back Yard"

"Hugh has provided a brilliantly simple strategy that creates wealth for the homeowner, tax-free, which adds even more value to the process. This book is easy to follow, organized and comprehensive."
      - Ralph Hahmann, Account Executive
      Cartier Partners

"Hugh Carter has taken the mysterious process of rezoning and subdividing and simplified them so that even the inexperienced person can follow each step along the way. This book enables the reader to understand and implement the information needed to create a new building lot. I recommend it highly to real estate agents and to property owners."
      - Helen Hones, B. Ed.
      JonesCo Real Estate Inc.

"Hugh Carter has created a book that enables the layperson to easily understand the rezoning and subdivision process. His use of before and after models is excellent. I highly recommend his book to everyone interested in rezoning and subdividing."
      - Dave Lunt, Certified Residential Designer
      Ted Lunt Designs Ltd.

"There is money in housing. Hugh Carter is a wealthy plumber. Just like the character in David Chilton's financial guide **The Wealthy Barber**, he did it using a simple and straightforward strategy."
      - Victoria Times Colonist
      Susan Down, Jan. 2001

Hidden Profits In Your Back Yard

Order Form

Is there someone you know who could benefit from reading **Pension Paradigm** and/or **Hidden Profits In Your Backyard**? They make the perfect gift.

☐ Yes, I'd like to purchase _____ copy(s) of **Pension Paradigm** for only $20.00

                                                     Amount _____

☐ Yes, I'd like to purchase_____ copy(s) of **Hidden Profits In Your Backyard** for only $20.00

                                         Amount _____

(Prices include shipping, handling and taxes)

                                        TOTAL _____

Name:_____

Address:_____

City:_____Prov:_____Postal Code:_____

Phone:(   )_____   Fax:(   )_____

☐ Attached is a cheque made payable to: Hugh Carter

or

Please bill: ☐ Visa   ☐ Master Card

Card Number:_____Expiry Date:_____

Cardholder Name:_____

Signature:_____

To order by fax, send this form to: (250) 383-8092
To order by email, contact: info@dhcarter.com
To order by mail, send this form to:

Hugh Carter, 356 Gorge Road East, Victoria, BC V8T 2W2
Please allow 1-4 weeks for delivery.